# Perspectives of Hope

*A Rescue Pilot's Silent Struggle to Find Life
Beyond PTSD, TBI and War*

## ROBERT SCOGGINS

ISBN: 978-1-948638-42-5

Front cover credits: Original painting by Robert Scoggins, photography by Paul Horton of PH Photo

**On the back cover:** Dee lands our crew's first mission of the day in support of COP Nolen (documented in Chapter 3). Soldiers with the US Army's 1-320 Field Artillery Regiment, 101st Airborne Division shield themselves from the dust as a Medevac helicopter lands outside Combat Outpost Nolen in the Arghandab Valley north of Kandahar July 30, 2010. One soldier lost his leg and another was hit by shrapnel after an Improvised Explosive Device (IED) blew up during a patrol near the base. REUTERS/Bob Strong

SAF/PA Approved Security Clearance Case Number 2018-0645 (2017-0344). Title Approval/Doc 30 Apr 2019. Please contact usaf.pentagon. saf-pa.mbx.saf-pa-security-and-policy-review@mail.mil.

Published by

Fideli Publishing, Inc.
119 W. Morgan St.
Martinsville, IN 46151

www.FideliPublishing.com

PRINTED IN THE UNITED STATES OF AMERICA

# DEDICATION

To my Brothers- and Sisters-in-Arms:

This book was written for those who have no idea what to think of their scars; those who live at odds with their own experiences; those who cannot understand how to let go and learn to live; and for the families trapped by their love, intimately familiar with an endless cycle of hope, anxiety, fear, anger, and depression. Most especially, this work is for the mothers and fathers who can no longer speak to their children.

# INSPIRATION

To the one dedicated to me:

This book was inspired by the one who saw goodness in me; the one who recognized the love and light trapped inside while I was fearful of showing anything but darkness to the world; the one who battled my ego and led us both to our truth. You have saved my life more than once, in more ways than I knew needed saving. This book is, and I still am, because of you. I give you my eternal love and gratitude, Jacqueline.

# ACKNOWLEDGEMENTS

For the amazing people at the Air Force Wounded Warrior Program, thank you. Frankly, I had so little trust left that I had to be talked into accepting your help. Somehow though, your tireless efforts restored my faith in, well, everyone.

In addition to a new lease on life, you have blessed me with something that is intangible, immeasurable, and far greater than any single moment could ever be by itself. I have found no term that could ever describe this experience, so I have had to create one: Generational Impact. My children and grandchildren will never know how different their lives are because of you, how much better, which is perhaps the richest gift of all. I am now and will forever be grateful for your unwavering support.

A special thank you to Rock to Recovery, Wesley Geer, and each of the unbelievable musicians you serve others alongside daily. Most especially Brandon Parkhurst, thank you for diving into the pain with me. A trapped soul can see nothing but brick walls and iron bars in every direction. For a long time, that defined me, and nothing was good enough to bother attempting. Having an unexpected wave of motivation, love and laughter burst through in an ever-present harmony is undeniable, as is the rhythm pouring from each of your hearts. Music truly is the medicine.

Wounded Warrior Project is perhaps the farthest-reaching, most impactful organization that I can never thank enough. Every event, activity, and Veteran in your employment has had a tremendously positive effect on my life. Perhaps this is my biggest testimony to your success — in less than a year of being out of service, I had transferred nearly every personal mental health recovery or treatment of mine into a program run, financed, or referred by your outstanding non-profit. Personal therapy, individual Veteran trips, marriage retreats, family events, and an intensive outpatient PTSD/TBI program have helped transform my *Why* into *How*.

Operation Mend is that intensive outpatient program, although the word *intensive* falls short of how life-changing the program and its vision are. I've experienced plate tectonics in an actual earthquake before, and there is no better comparison between that motion and my internal transitions post-*Mend*. The doctors, therapists, and staff devoted to this mission are my absolute heroes. Dr. Valuzzi, Dr. Treanor, and every colleague of yours I was blessed to grow from have inarguably captured the evasive spirit that C. J. Jung coined as *unprejudiced objectivity*. Thank you all for treating my wife and me without judgement, expectation, or anything other than complete, untarnished love for another human being.

Veterans to Farmers, Richard Murphy, Jamie Wickler, anyone and everyone else associated with your wonderful non-profit, thank you for your education, guidance, and friendship. The image brought by a little known term, *soul tribe*, completely defines what this group embodies to many of us. Your examples are shining lights, and I am so grateful for the life that radiance is leading me towards.

Karen Elliott, of Rocky Mountain Labradoodles, donated me a service dog. I have yet to find the words to describe what this kindness has done. I didn't even realize for a long time that the gift came before knowing a single detail about me. How does one give so freely of themselves, of their own livelihood? How could another care so much for a stranger that this spontaneity was ever an option? I asked a close friend these same questions and the simple answer was, "That's God."

A special thank you to Semper Fi/America's Fund, Wounded Warrior Family Support, Our Military Kids, Operation Home-front, Hearts of Valor, Quality of Life Foundation, Team R4V, CAMMO, the Cohen Veterans Network, and the Elizabeth Dole Foundation. I can never repay what has been done for me or my family, so I must accept a life of always attempting to match your standards. Every act of kindness I have received will be put back out three-fold. Quite simply, you all are the raddest people I have ever known.

There is a time-tested proverb that says, *Give a man a fish, feed him for a day. Teach a man to fish, feed him for a lifetime.* I would officially like to add, *Inspire a man to hope, so that you may feast upon his creations.*

For the privilege of your time and for the inspiration that each has given me, thank you all, and thank you again.

# TABLE OF CONTENTS

# PREFACE

Hello. My name is Robert, and I am an addict.

You see, I used to think I was an alcoholic, but I've since realized any impulsive behavior is something I crave. Adrenaline, sex, caffeine, painkillers, porn? Yes, please. Anything that keeps my mind off of reality works. Anxiety, depression, self-hatred, reckless behavior, defensive rage? I can't put them down. Hardcore narcotics? No thanks, I'm addicted to control, or at least the illusion of it.

Some of you may know what I mean when I say I went to combat, and since then, things...stopped making sense. To be more precise, I didn't fit in like I used to.

Sleep? Sure, I had pills to sleep. Nightmares would wake me up a matter of hours later, though. Headaches? Of course, but that was no problem. I'd take two Motrin 800 mg (or vitamin M, as they're known in the flying world), two maximum strength Tylenol, wash them down with coffee, swallow an alternating dose of both every couple of hours, then drink energy soda until switching to alcohol.

That was just the visible fraction of the cycle I found myself living following my time in Afghanistan. I recognized I needed help, but asking for it didn't change anything. I bounced from one therapist to the next, knowing I required more but not allowing it, because for an Air Force pilot, full disclosure means losing your career.

When I finally quit caring about the consequences of admitting my problems (because the consequences of living in misery were much worse), I found many people who were there to assist, through no fault of their own, had no clue how to do this. I became strung out and hopeless to the point I attempted suicide, at first passively, then actively.

When that failed, I had to face the hard truth and give up my excuses. All of them. I had to admit to myself that I couldn't stop. The anger, the confusion, the aggression, I couldn't stop any of it. None of it was my fault. Everything was my fault. I had to learn acceptance, and I had no idea I hadn't done that when confessing I needed treatment.

It turns out going to a mental health professional was unrelated to accepting I had mental health issues. Accepting meant I must become aware and deal with my symptoms in each moment, as if they were brand new every time.

So, when did I get to this point? If you asked the people close to me, the answer would vary. To some family members and friends, the changes were noticeable the second I returned from war. Those people, no matter who they were, were cut out of my life not long after they questioned me. Others had no idea, as in, they were around me often for more than half a decade and had no clue I was struggling. They were quite confused when I decided to give up my lifestyle of external coping.

The funny part about this is that somewhere along the way my story converges with that of many Veterans. This book started out as my narrative, but in reality, my problems manifested so similarly to others that this could be called *our* narrative. And it points to the exact same ending: the main character dying alone.

As for my estranged family members and friends, some wrote me off as a complete jerk, while others claimed I'd always been that way. I often heard my behavior was an excuse to do whatever I wanted.

I've heard these common themes many times about other Veterans. *Yeah, he came back different. But he was always an asshole...*

The man quoted was talking about his own twin brother, whom he had not spoken to in more than three years. That's just how easily a human being can be written off. I wish I'd taken more notes, it is that heart-breaking.

I haven't spoken to (or even known how to speak to) many of my family members in years. There's no way to force another to not judge or question, and holding onto the same lifestyle, albeit through hidden coping, was no longer an option for me. I was unable to apologize and go back to being who they expected me to be. How could a loved one not notice or ask?

The difficult part is others aren't wrong for misunderstanding. Many people cannot or will not ever be open to learning. Most wouldn't even know what that would look like.

Post-Traumatic Stress Disorder (PTSD) is an anxiety disorder caused after experiencing a terrifying event (or events), sometimes involving exposure to death, threat of death, or severe physical injuries/wounds. This results in physiological changes within the brain. The mind changes in composition as it grows in real time to get better at counteracting any possible threat. Areas of the brain that concentrate on reactions or self-defense become physically larger, while other areas stay the same size, or even shrink.

A human being with PTSD reacts differently to the environment and everyone in it. Any situation, noise, image, smell, memory, or pattern perceived may cause an emotional response for people without an anxiety disorder. However, with this disorder, if that emotion is anywhere close to the feelings experienced in the inciting event(s), the result may be catastrophic.

For those suffering with PTSD, the same fight or flight response felt in the past becomes alive in the present, demanding action, defense, or safety. Anger is thrown out at random times toward anyone or anything as a pre-emptive measure. Miscommunications become the norm, and the desire for control consistently overpowers as trust decreases to all-time lows.

In the early stages, the symptoms from the disorder may not be evident. Life may even continue for a while without much changing for the individual, as far as outward appearances go. Eventually, maintaining the semblance of "normal" becomes so exhausting that avoidance becomes the favored tune for many.

Excessive dependence on coping methods can turn into isolation or addictions of all kinds. Even healthy activities, such as religion, exercise, work, or food may turn into a destructive pattern. The desire to control everything and everyone in the vicinity usually takes over as these conditioned behaviors become more overwhelming than instinct.

No, I do not sit around all day seeing dead people. But the physical changes within the brain, combined with the reality of today's warfare, means that emotions cannot be trusted until I've examined them with careful detachment.

This is because variables of every type have been woven into the experiences. Up-to-the-minute communication means 30 minutes removed from a firefight, I could've been getting lectured about missed e-mails or late personnel reports, dealing with sick kids, sprinting back into the heat of battle, taking cover from air raid sirens, or balancing monthly budgets to stay ahead of day-to-day financial worries.

Annoyances about oppressive conditions, blocking thoughts of dead friends, and living through occasional terror as one fights to stay alive combines the memories of those with PTSD into a kind of twisted alternate reality that may take years to untangle. The only question is, how does life become re-defined during the detangling process?

For Veterans with PTSD, identity, pride, guilt, successes, failures, and every extreme emotion have become tied together in the most unique way. There is no one-size-fits-all-cure. To live again, we each must take charge of our own recovery and demand growth in a new direction, because nobody else could ever know how we got to where we are.

This book was written to explain that which cannot be explained. I've opened myself up to provide a look into life post-combat and to offer a subconscious perspective of how I got to the point of suicide. I pray that by sharing a glimpse into my struggles, I may offer understanding to families and friends who are hurting in their own ways.

But there is another piece to this puzzle. Writing began as a way for me to understand and deal with my repressed emotions resulting from combat. I didn't know why I was systematically dismantling my life, or even that it was happening. In retrospect, however, it's clear that I did it to myself, no one else. It's also obvious that I'll be trapped in my homemade cycle of hell until I can process it all and learn how to forgive, both myself and others.

It is my sincere hope that, if nothing else is accomplished with this book, the reader will better understand the emotional and spiritual trauma Veterans experience, for with understanding comes forgiveness.

# INTRODUCTION

On February 17, 2009, the President of the United States signed an executive order that sent an additional 17,000 U.S. troops to Afghanistan. This was on top of the 36,000 U.S. and 32,000 International Security Assistance Force (ISAF) service members already there.

Despite this increase, U.S. military leadership predicted the almost decade-long war would be lost within a year if there wasn't another significant influx of troops. On December 1, 2009, an additional 30,000 soldiers, sailors, marines, and airmen were ordered to the Afghani theater.

A substantial number of these forces were directed to the southern districts of Helmand and Khandahar provinces. In early 2010, the first offensive of the surge began in the insurgent-dominated town of Marjah, in the heart of the Helmand Province.

Accompanying the change of direction in this nine-year-old war were a new set of orders that were the opposite of what most service members expected to hear. The mandatory policy, sent to all troops before the first surge, was to hold fire whenever possible.

"Winning Hearts and Minds" was the actual campaign slogan for this 2010 Afghanistan troop surge, and it soon became the mantra of victory for the entire war. This resulted in U.S. service members decreasing their defensive ability and posture by holding fire more often, while increasing patrols outside defensive positions more frequently and in greater numbers.

Translation? Thousands of U.S. ground troops were sent to patrol local villages, farmers' fields, and major lines of communication, while holding fire until fired upon. Combined with a new influx of tactics and lessons learned from enemy forces in Iraq, Afghani insurgents were compelled to instigate fighting with an increased vigor not seen before.

This equation spelled disaster, especially for ground convoys (multiple armored vehicles following each other in a column stretching almost as far as railway trains) where the enemy was able to choose the time and location for any confrontation.

In the southern, agriculture-centric, provinces of Khandahar and Helmand, three helicopter units were assigned to Khandahar Airfield and Camp Bastion, respectively, to rescue any American or ISAF service members. An Army helicopter medevac (medical evacuation) unit covered half of Khandahar Airfield's medical flights, and a British helicopter medevac unit shared a portion of Camp Bastion's.

One Air Force Combat Rescue squadron, my unit, carried the other half of the load at both locations. We tasked a handful of helicopters and four crews each to 24/7 rescue operations at Khandahar and Bastion. Two crews covered the A.M. shift, and another two flew the P.M. hours. Our callsign, PEDRO, soon became our identity. It was the only name any of us assumed or ever declared while flying, and it was cherished more than the label of a New York Yankee or Dallas Cowboy could ever hope.

Always flying in a formation, or flight, of two helicopters, our crews operated the HH-60G Sikorsky PaveHawk helicopters, which carried two pilots, a Flight Engineer (FE), and a gunner, both of whom manned a .50 caliber side mounted weapon. When arriving on-scene, one of us would fly overhead as the cover aircraft, capable of air-ground fire support, while the other landed to perform the rescue.

Split between both aircraft, we also carried a ParaRescue team of five operators (trained to a Paramedic Certification level) plus their personal weapons and medical gear. All told, our HH-60G helicopters had room and weight available for a handful of injured or wounded, always known to the crews as, our patients.

Summer through Fall of 2010, my crew flew the morning shift, at first in Khandahar as callsign PEDRO 55. We then swapped to finish our tour in Camp Bastion as PEDRO 23. At each location, we had a spare helicopter or two, a handful of extra aircrew, an overworked maintenance unit, and a few operations staff to somehow put the whole thing together.

Our squadron was a combined unit, primarily made up of airmen deployed from three separate stateside squadrons. Due to the requirements of the Iraq and Afghanistan wars, our squadrons had been replacing themselves in both theaters for the majority of the last decade. Roughly half of the 100–200-man squadrons stayed home (unit size is dependent upon the aircraft assigned at each location), while the rest were deployed to Iraq or Afghanistan as necessary. The aircrew at home flew training missions while preparing to take the place of those downrange, usually in a matter of months.

Most of the airmen in my unit lived a one-on/one-off/one-on deployment schedule for years. This lifestyle wasn't easy, but it illustrates some of the reasons why our career field takes so much pride in the Combat Rescue Motto: *These Things We Do, That Others May Live.*

Although I didn't start my Air Force career in rescue, it certainly was the path I'd set myself towards from the beginning. Growing up in a small Georgia town, I'd always wanted to be a pilot. Having a long and proud family history of military service, I never bothered to look for any avenue to the skies outside of the Air Force. I was thrilled when I earned a scholarship to an army-based junior college my senior year of high school, followed by an acceptance to the U.S. Air Force Academy a year later.

Most 18-year-olds wouldn't be excited by the prospect of spending a year studying and training with the Army in backwoods Alabama. Many thought I was nuts when I explained that success, for me, would be defined by living another four years in a military academy, all just to fly. However, I plain loved it...not the late nights, the lock-downs, and certainly not the constant control. But the camaraderie, the friendships, the bizarre things that could never happen anywhere else, these things made the difficult times worth it.

When I finally finished my fifth year of military college, I had indeed earned a pilot training slot and was sent to helicopters following two years of flight training. (On an ironic note, had I stuck with the Army after junior college instead, I could've been flying operationally at least two years earlier.) As things were, I was happy with my lot in life when our crew headed out the door to Khandahar Airfield, Afghanistan, in June of 2010.

I was flying as the mission pilot in the left seat with a good friend, Dee, as the aircraft commander and Flight Lead in the right seat. Andy, our gunner, sat behind me, and the Flight Engineer, Brack, sat opposite. Andy and Brack manned nearly identical .50 caliber machine guns. For this reason, we didn't fly with the traditional medevac Red Cross painted on the cabin doors, like our Army counterparts did.

Assigned to the Flying Tigers, the same unit my maternal grandfather had flown with in World War II, our group mindset was forged with the aggression and tone the Flying Tigers' shark teeth brought to China in the 1940s. We never said no and tolerated nothing less than complete and total commitment to the patient and the mission. Anything and everything that attempted to get in the way could, quite simply, go fuck itself.

Living and fighting in such a pressure-cooker situation causes different changes to each individual that can never be predicted. Barely weeks after this deployment, I had extreme difficulty even being around my two children. Months removed from Afghanistan, I'd initiated a divorce and was working toward a full-blown alcoholic lifestyle. Within five years, I found myself incapable of ever flying again, awaiting separation from the service, and becoming more suicidal by the day.

So, how did I get to that point? To acknowledge my PTSD and traumatic brain injury (TBI) diagnoses and then move on would be the simplest course of action. Yet, that would be so incomplete as to be totally inaccurate.

PTSD is not a linear disorder, it's based upon an emotionally patterned, or repetitive timeline. It has been labeled a disorder of non-recovery, because the affected person usually can't escape a cycle of self-destructive behavior without entering or using a slightly different spiral of avoidance, a coping source, or a combination of the two. This is due to an intense focus on the trauma and false concepts learned that send the mind back in circles over and again.

The patterns of life are different for each person with PTSD, as the symptoms develop based upon an individual's experience and his or her subsequent changes in judgment. The ability to make good decisions for oneself, unfortunately, is what may be most affected by the disorder.

For instance, emotional reasoning has been my greatest challenge for years now. That fact alone indicates not everyone would fall into my exact category. This deficit turned me into an unaware hypocrite, constantly using poor emotional judgements based upon things felt in the moment instead of personal values or life goals to make my decisions (no matter how major or minor).

The big-picture similarities, the patterns of life that were evident in me, are unmistakable, undeniable, and on some level, parallel to so many others afflicted with PTSD. Those cycles would become evident as I climbed out of one hole, only to find myself falling into another repetition of similar self-destructive behavior.

The risk-taking soon added up to create an indisputable picture of deliberateness. Passive attempts at taking my own life emerged as I would randomly jump out of a car or walk through traffic. One month before my discharge from the Air Force, my first active and last real attempt at killing myself occurred.

During that suicide attempt, I learned some things through what can only be called a flashback. I saw how intricately connected, how tightly entwined, all of my memories and experiences are. That flashback, that gift of perspective, is my story.

And I thank you for reading.

# PAVEHAWK FLIGHT CONTROLS

CYCLIC (a.k.a. Stick) - Controls tilt of rotor disc (direction of lift and thrust). Works the same as an airplane.

COLLECTIVE (a.k.a. Torque or Power) - Controls rotor pitch/angle (thrust, lift, engine RPM)

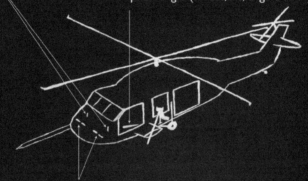

ANTI-TORQUE (a.k.a. Tail Rotor Pedals) - Controls tail rotor pitch/angle (turns aircraft in a hover, streamlines yaw during forward flight)

*PaveHawk flight controls.*

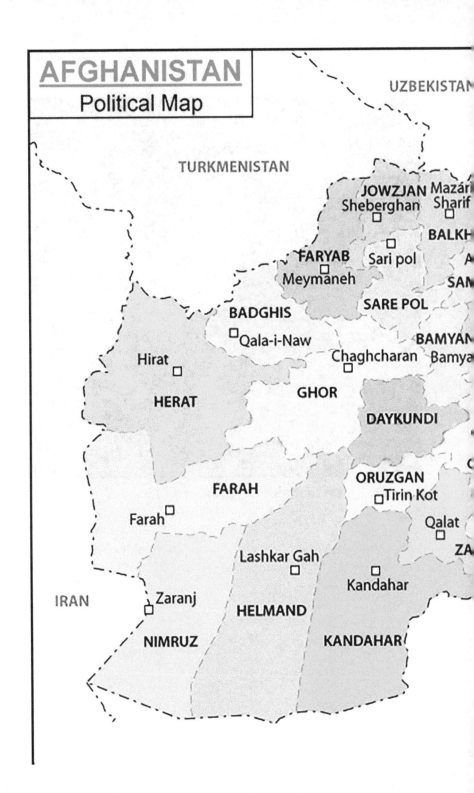

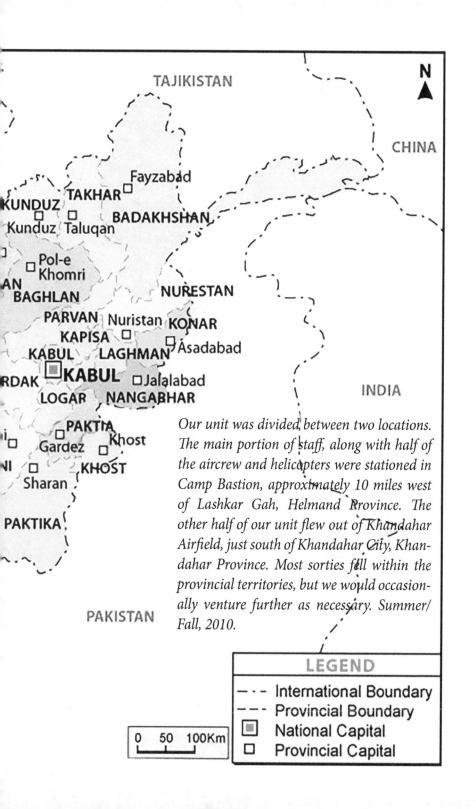

TAJIKISTAN

CHINA

N

Fayzabad

TAKHAR

KUNDUZ
Kunduz Taluqan

BADAKHSHAN

Pol-e
Khomri

AN
BAGHLAN

NURESTAN

PARVAN Nuristan KONAR

KAPISA

KABUL LAGHMAN Asadabad

RDAK KABUL Jalalabad

INDIA

LOGAR NANGARHAR

PAKTIA

i Gardez Khost

NI KHOST

Sharan

PAKTIKA

PAKISTAN

*Our unit was divided between two locations. The main portion of staff, along with half of the aircrew and helicopters were stationed in Camp Bastion, approximately 10 miles west of Lashkar Gah, Helmand Province. The other half of our unit flew out of Khandahar Airfield, just south of Khandahar City, Khandahar Province. Most sorties fell within the provincial territories, but we would occasionally venture further as necessary. Summer/ Fall, 2010.*

LEGEND

— · — International Boundary
— — — Provincial Boundary
▣ National Capital
□ Provincial Capital

0  50  100Km

# CHAPTER 1

# A PERMANENT SOLUTION

## LAS VEGAS, NEVADA, FALL, 2015

**H**ate. I am hate. I hate everything and everyone.

"How did this happen?" I pathetically voiced. "How in the...?"

I suppose any free-fall has to stop at some point. I tried prayer not long after learning I needed to go to a formal court hearing to prove I'd served in combat, but nothing seemed to improve. In fact, things kept getting worse.

I sat in my beautiful master suite bathroom, locked securely in a self-built mental prison, serving time on cheap beige carpet. Surrounded by nothing but bland drywall, nondescript plaster, and sterile bathroom white, I was disgusted by the mirror's empty reflection.

The face looked familiar, sure. Light brown hair, some freckles, and a few scars were there, just as before. But the differences were shocking. My formerly muscular, six-foot, one-inch, 200-pound frame had been whittled down to a buck sixty. Any semblance of laughter had fled long before like rats from a sinking ship. Whenever I hit rock bottom, it was going to hurt like hell.

Our house was 4,700 square feet of grandeur on a sprawling half-acre, complete with a casita and a three-stall garage full of toys, including a Harley and a BMW. A massive Ram 3500 truck lifted on top of polished 35-inch tires sat in the driveway. I hated all of it.

During one of my recent fits, I'd become so enraged I threw my Harley into the BMW, and its after-market handlebars punched straight through the passenger door. The emptiness of purpose in that garage was a metaphor for what I'd become. Echoes of so-called life-lessons shrilled out like nails on a chalkboard: promises of the good life, of the American dream. These arbitrary thoughts brought no relief from the pain.

For years my mind had played a game with me. It insisted danger was nearby and I needed to find it. This used to mean I'd get into frequent arguments, unintentionally taking every misunderstanding like a threat to my very existence. As I became more aware of myself, and more afraid, I hadn't left the house except for a handful of times in months.

The more I isolated myself, however, the more my thoughts transitioned toward anger at society in general. The negative emotions seemed to manifest anywhere, at any time. And instead of doing me any good, this type of thinking sent me down the wrong path, as I yet again mentally circled the drain.

*All of it is a lie, my whole life...brainwashed into slavery.* I stared through my reflection with no clear purpose for this knowledge. Feelings of betrayal, rejection, frustration, and confusion swirled overhead in a dark cloud, building as they fed upon my every thought.

*Brainwashed into giving my entire life, and thrown out like this...* I couldn't stand how my military career ended.

Standing and chortling out loud, I thought back on the sequence of events that had led me here.

*Okay, so you went a little crazy after Afghanistan... Had you not totaled that SUV with your face in 2011, nothing would've come of it.* My mind argued self-blame inside its own dialogue as I thought of the motorcycle wreck that led to my brain injury.

*Africa, that one hurt.* I switched mental pictures to my last deployment. Shortly before coming home in March of 2013, I woke to an e-mail notifying me I was being transferred from piloting combat rescue helicopters to flying drones. Or, as I'd come to view it, being re-directed from my personal calling of saving lives to killing via remote control.

Not long before I received that message, I was involved in the planning and rescue of a prisoner that went haywire. One member of the rescue team was captured and then executed, along with our hostage.

Wandering down the air-conditioned hallway of my large home, I stopped at the top of the stairs. I'd once pictured this winding staircase surrounding a tall Christmas tree, under which excited kids opened presents.

*I'm pretty sure I've torched that possibility, too.* My mind orbited a black hole of anger and absolute gravity, as I felt heavier and heavier. Succumbing to weakness, my body dropped down on the fifth step. Visions of the past year and a half flashed faster in sequence while my weight seemingly corresponded to the mental depths I was falling into.

*Please kill me,* I begged nobody, putting the plea out there, nonetheless.

A good friend's death and the loss of her entire crew had kicked off 2014. On my way home from the funeral, having no clue as to why I was so furious, I found myself meandering through the Las Vegas airport traffic tunnel and down the Interstate before being picked up by Las Vegas Metro Police.

Three months later, I was permanently grounded from flying for crying in the base mental health office. I spent months at work afterwards, isolated in a dark, windowless office, reviewing useless paperwork.

This desk job was explained, "...so you can still be useful to the government." Orders are rarely accompanied with such cold, precise reasoning.

Patterns of erratic behavior, alcoholic binges, and damaging self-hate emerged as my only coping strategies. To make matters worse, a serious sports injury re-introduced me to the opiate addiction I'd barely managed to escape after the motorcycle crash.

I'd grown up playing competitive soccer in Georgia before playing three years of intercollegiate rugby at the Air Force Academy. This injury ended sports for me. The idea of having no healthy physical outlet ever again felt closer to a death sentence than anything else.

In 2015, I sunk into a severe depression during the 18-month Air Force Medical Evaluation Board process. This board would determine my entire future, how and when I left the service and what I would legally be allowed to do...or not do...as a pilot for the rest of my life. Unbeknownst to me, my service records had been improperly transferred and disregarded. Having to prepare a court defense to prove my combat service felt like shame personified.

*Dan's suicide was right after...* I reminded myself.

In less than one year's time, our rescue community had lost another four-helicopter aircrew to their own hands. Without any notice, desire, or initiative on my part, suicide had suddenly become a prominent factor in my life.

A VA official's warning in March of 2015 had almost driven my wife insane. "Ten people in this med board process kill themselves each month…"

I never actually contemplated suicide until a little while later, but I was sure this speech hadn't helped.

The non-stop memories were as difficult to keep up with as they were random. I kept getting angrier as the waves of emotion took hold of my cognitive protests and silenced any coherent reasoning. My mind skipped ahead to recent history.

Embarrassment hit like a tidal wave as I remembered one of the last times I'd hung out with friends that summer. At a fundraiser, something set me off, and I tried to leave. Somehow, a buddy's wife thought she'd upset me and wanted to apologize. However, once her hand touched my shoulder, I threw her across the parking lot. I allowed almost no one around me after that.

Anger for everything else was soon turned on myself. *I can't do anything about any of it…*

The shame that had just appeared transitioned back to fury at my very existence with the flip of a switch. Useless and destructive, that anger was not satisfied without some kind of physical response.

My body acted as if programmed. I took the stairs down two at a time. Rushing into the hall, I began hitting the drywall, attacking it repeatedly, not knowing why and incapable of asking or stopping. The emotions were that overwhelming.

*Crunch!*

I smashed my hand punching a wooden stud. Rather than stop, I became more furious and walloped it again, jamming every tiny bone in my hand in the process. The next steps were a blur as off-white walls flashed by. I had no idea where I was going but still rushed to get there.

I suddenly found myself in a front spare room, staring at my open gun safe. Sunlight leaked through the stark white blinds, lighting up dust motes in the unused space.

*Why am I holding my pistol? Who taught me this? What am I doing?* The protests of my soul had long been silenced.

I hadn't believed in God or anything religious since I could remember. Prayer did nothing for me. Come to think of it, I doubted I'd ever felt any spiritual knowing or connection to church.

I was breathing hard, shaking even more, and only a couple of seconds away from hyperventilating. Looking at the gun I held, I ran my quivering finger down the slide one last time. I paused as I felt the laser-etched partial engraving of our Combat Rescue Motto, ... *That Others May Live.*

That phrase used to have meaning for me. Once upon a time I was a part of something. I used to be a combat rescue helicopter pilot. That's right, the Air Force actually employs a few hundred of us stupid enough to love helicopters.

Achievements and accolades from that past life used to hold substance. Today, I hated those words and numbers with a passion that outweighed my love for anything else: Iraq, Afghanistan, Africa, 252 combat missions, 291 rescues and recoveries, 151 lives saved.

Those numbers were supposed to bring me pride. The term *Lives Saved* was applied because of the severity of the wound, the injury, or the situation. We were given a timeline of one hour to make the rescue from the time we were called until we landed at the hospital pad...regardless of who tried to kill us en route.

*Yeah, right, 151 before they were put into this... How many of them are dead now? How many killed themselves rather than continue like this?* These thoughts used to keep me up nights.

For a long time, I'd survived in a sick cycle of drinking, crying, and writing e-mails to former patients. I would usually delete the messages before sending, too afraid to learn the truth.

These thoughts now included a morbid realization: *Some of those guys killed themselves, anyway. So many more of our patients are dead today...*

This was to be the third and final decision about my own suicide. I'd quit drinking cold turkey more than a year before, but life had gotten worse. I'd grown so exhausted and ashamed from not understanding my emotional outbursts that I hardly ever left the house.

No one ever told me PTSD would mostly make me angry. I never knew a traumatic brain injury would cause me to act like a toddler at times, yet appear fine otherwise, with few cognitive issues at all. Life was too embarrassing without alcohol or something else to obsess about. No matter what I drank or didn't drink, what drug I was on or wasn't, I lost control of my emotional reasoning on average three to four times a week.

I had no idea who I was anymore; I'd felt no identity in so long. The last time I thought about killing myself, a good friend showed up outside my house and sat in the heat for hours, even though I never let him in. But I knew he was there, so I couldn't go through with it.

This time, I'd driven my wife so far away I was certain nobody would be called. That was what I wanted, that was what I needed...

I stepped up to the plate one last time, flipping the safety down on my already-cocked Sig Sauer 1911 pistol and put the barrel to my head. Stuck using my left hand, I wasn't used to the strange feel of the gun.

"No matter either way," I muttered. "One more Vet."

Not very poetic, I admit, but at this point I'd already married myself to the idea of not living like this for another moment.

Little pressure is required on any 1911 when the hammer is already cocked. It truly is a beautiful weapon, known for reliability. The .45 caliber rounds have enough stopping power to drop anyone.

"Hate, hate, hate..." I pulled the trigger, dropping the hammer down, putting firing pin to primer, not knowing if I'd even hear the crack.

*...to be continued...*

# CHAPTER 2

# INTRUSIVE THOUGHTS

## MANAS AIR BASE, KYRGYZSTAN, FALL 2010
*(Five years earlier)*

*RACK!*

*Holy shit! Loud damn kids.* I mentally cursed the noise coming from the Marines on the other side of the tent, sat up on the old green cot, and checked my watch. *What time is it?*

*Let's see, if it's 3:20 a.m. in Helmand, is it 4:50 a.m. here?* I answered my own question with another unknown. The sheer magnitude of simple math left me even more confused. The only thing I was certain of was that recent history was a complete and total blur.

I'd woken up two days before at Camp Bastion, a British Forward Operating Base in Helmand Province, Afghanistan. Not knowing anything about how the day would end, I stuck to the same routine as always: sleep for a few hours, work out in a tent until midnight, link up with the other three members of my crew, and then prepare flight gear and weapons at the aircraft.

Next, we had a changeover brief at 2 a.m. including us, our wingman's crew, and the two outgoing crews we were replacing before officially taking over our rescue alert shift for the next 12 hours. We never had any idea where we'd end up, but, as our inside joke went, *wherever the scariest environment imaginable is.*

Somehow I'd ended up here, frozen and alone in this transient dump a day and a half later. *I don't even have travel orders, do I?*

No orders home, no gear, no weapons, and no crew. I turned to my bag like there could be a single thing in it that I hadn't packed myself.

*Still a no... Why is that funny?* I laughed as I laid back down, closed my eyes, and answered my own question again, muttering, *Fuck it.*

I avoided worrying about whether I could catch a flight home and worried instead about sleeping over the noise. *Probably not.*

I opened my eyes, for good this time, having realized I was fooling myself. No way could I sleep when my body was used to playing poker or rummaging through our alert tent (or alert shack, as it was known at our Khandahar location) for food, enjoying the last few hours until daylight. The tent, or shack, was nothing more than a slightly less dusty place to stick our two crews close to the helicopters while sitting on alert, waiting for the first rescue call, usually not long after sunrise.

*Sun's Out, Guns Out.* That old frat boy t-shirt expression took on an entirely different meaning in the Afghani Helmand River Valley, also known as the Green Zone.

Shaking off the daze, I realized I'd been awake for 33 hours and, judging by the 20 or so Marines playing grab-ass like it was Christmas morning, I wasn't going to sleep until I caught the rotator home (a contracted commercial airline flight that ferries troops from the U.S. to these transient bases).

I sat up on my cot inside our freezing tent in frigid Asskrackistan, swore at the cold, and pulled my boots on. Between

Iraq, Las Vegas, and Afghanistan, I hadn't felt this kind of frigid temperature extreme in years.

*Ass-krackistan, that joke sucks.* I attempted to amuse myself at my own expense. If nothing else, it helped pass the time.

Looking around at at the old, worn-out tent these Marines and I were calling home, I tried not to think about my crew as I played with the dirt on my two-piece tan flight suit that I'd been wearing for months. They'd just taken over the alert shift, which wasn't much more than sitting in the tent, waiting for the first *Scramble* to be called. (*Scramble* was our single command over the radio network that ordered us immediately to the aircraft.)

*Maybe there's a dust storm over Helmand today. Maybe they'll sit alert and do nothing.* Pff, pff, pff. Tiny clouds of talcum powder floated off of my shirt as I flicked it, thinking of my friends.

These nervous ticks without consideration had long ago ceased to be habits and probably fell into a category titled *messed up twitches* or even *TSD*, as Brack, our Flight Engineer always joked. *PTSD means Post. TSD is for dudes already mental and still stuck here.*

*There.* I corrected myself. I half-laughed, half-choked, thinking of our crusty, old Flight Engineer.

*Man, my TSD is acting up again.* The dialogue played out in my head, the way it had every single day in the alert tent for the past six months. I wasn't positive, but I was pretty sure the eight of us in both crews had developed some stupid reaction to the squelch of our alert bricks (black walky-talky-style radios in the shape of bricks whose sole purpose was to galvanize our two helicopter crews into battle).

The most frequent, and embarrassing, response was falling asleep in the alert tent and waking up in a dead sprint out the door, simultaneously terrified and confused, as your closest friends laughed their asses off at you. That had happened to me at least a dozen times, and there was no other way to describe it. *TSD.*

I realized I'd been zoning out while staring at the dim utility lamp swinging in our group tent, so I tried to shake off the daze. I looked at my watch, for the millionth time, before being taken over again by my drifting thoughts, *It's 5:30 a.m.... Maybe my crew won't...*

*Shut up!* I shouted at myself, and as quick as I could, I compartmentalized. *Fuck that place! Fuck this place! Fuck this life!*

Being so tired, my mind was a lot harder to control than normal, and it meandered intermittently to my children as I took in my surroundings another countless time. *My son is almost two years old, and I've missed so much.*

Piles of gear lay stacked on the Marines' cots while they celebrated with each other the joy that, in a transient base, means one thing: going home. I wasn't mad at them. I got it. Had my situation been different, I would've been partying too.

As if to remind me of the dark days in which I was living, the rhythm of the chilly wind outside picked up its intensity. The sides and top of the 50-man bedroom whipped around, causing waves I could've translated into a riptide metaphor, had I been a little more steady.

*Two years old, and I've only seen him for...* My mind gave up avoiding the thoughts of my kids as I tried basic arithmetic instead. *Let's see, four and a half months plus three months. Do those five days after he was born round that half up to a full month?*

These pitiful attempts at justifying my fatherhood were rapidly overcome by reality. Vinegar-flavored bile rose up in my mouth as I opened Pandora's box.

*The doctors think it's Leukemia...* Tears now flowed freely as I wiped the disgusting taste on my sweat-stained, dirt-encrusted shirt.

I suppressed thoughts of my son deep into a place I'd never been before and concentrated on another favorite quote, *Coffee, stat!*

My mind drifted back to my friends, first to our Flight Engineer, Brack. Always speaking in a relaxed southern drawl, his laid-back five-foot, eleven-inch frame and easy-going laugh hid his serious nature. His dark brown eyes never missed a thing. Anytime someone stepped out of line around the helicopter, his verbal punishment came as swift as the trigger squeeze of his .50 caliber cannon. Brack's friendship and loyalty were never easily given or taken away, much like our other pilot, Dee.

*Dee is probably reading some hippy book right now.* An ear-to-ear grin spread over my face as the mental trick paid off.

I'd said these kinds of things to Dee's face out of love so many times I never bothered to include I was joking anymore. Weighing maybe 100 pounds soaking wet, she carried a chill, west coast demeanor mixed with an intensity that came from another planet. As the Flight Lead in charge of both helicopters and crews in our formation, this assertiveness was a quality Dee seldom needed to demonstrate within our crew.

Yesterday, this tiny flower child had to hold me up after I collapsed following the news about my son. Every single memory I carry from Afghanistan has her profile sitting in the right pilot seat.

"Mijo, you good?" Andy, our crew's gunner, arrived into my thoughts with a query.

The echo of Andy's voice was so loud I could almost hear him above the wind outside. His Mexican-American accent always showed when he was either messing around or pissed off, which covered a majority of our waking moments together. Although he sat maybe two feet behind me for the full deployment, I became accustomed to his voice in my helmet while only seeing him outside the aircraft.

I must've looked around the tent several minutes for my friend before lapsing into another vision of us either laughing with him or at him. All too often our days were filled with both. I completely loved that guy, all three of them actually.

The soundtrack to our friendships was filled with intercom squelches (the little scratches and beeps when a microphone switch is triggered), non-stop jokes, and a belief that we'd find a way through whatever was going on, no matter how impossible the situation seemed.

That image suddenly brought up the one thing I somehow felt but couldn't understand. *I am no longer part of my crew...*

*Just like Iraq before.* I lied to myself.

Nothing about Afghanistan was like Iraq, except for the fact that everyone wanted you dead. Strangely enough, the environment tended to kill more helicopter crews than any enemy ever could.

My mind finally stopped drifting and hit its target, sending me for the first time down a dark mental trap, *Why aren't we dead?*

* * *

> *For the first time I could remember, the complete envelop-*
> *ment of thoughts, emotions, and memories became part of my*
> *daily life. No matter the time, place, or date, any emotional tie*
> *could immediately send me into that experience. Musicians,*
> *artists, addicts, and many others illustrate that this is where*
> *the downward spiral begins. However, where it begins for me*
> *doesn't matter. In the end, I always wind up in the same place:*
> *Afghanistan, 2010.*

## CAMP BASTION, HELMAND PROVINCE, AFGHANISTAN, FALL, 2010
*(Two Days Prior)*

*SQUELCH...*

"*Scramble, Scramble, Scramble! All PEDRO'S Scramble!*" The all too-familiar radio command broke the boredom of our alert tent.

We usually heard nothing beyond that first squelch as the tent cleared. All eight of us aircrew and anyone else attached to our radio network were already at their stations or running full speed across the metal grates that formed the makeshift landing pads for our two HH-60G PaveHawk combat search and rescue helicopters.

This was a race against time. In less than an hour from the time of the call, we needed to be wheels down at the hospital pad with the wounded. I had no idea how the hell I'd ended up in one of the few units that literally sprinted into battle, but I'd be lying if I said I didn't love it.

For some reason, this part of the job had become a game months before. I used to approach launching the aircraft as intensely as death and taxes. However, as our crew got deeper into this deployment, caution had been thrown out the window. We now screwed around while running checklists in total synchronization, but strangely, this seemed to make us even faster.

Every step was completed, most from memory, while Brack, Andy, and I threw on our helmets and aircrew vests. These each weighed close to a metric shit-ton fully loaded: soft and hard body armor, almost a dozen ammunition pouches, a survival radio the size of a blender, tourniquets, and anything else you simply couldn't live without.

I draped myself in everything but the kitchen sink as I plugged into the radio system, known as comms, and strapped into the cockpit of PEDRO 23, our callsign as Flight Lead. (Lead's callsign is the only one used for both aircraft in the formation.) My checklists were completed through laughter as the other two talked trash to each other, halting only to drag me into the verbal melee.

"Are you still flappin' your gums?" Andy interrupted our checklists in his unique way of messing with me; he really knew how to crack me up.

Dee appeared last, running to the helicopter knock-kneed and goofy as hell. By this time, she'd figured out we went hysterical enjoying the ridiculous way she ran. To her credit, since hearing this, she often made it much worse, just for our benefit.

"Here she comes, galloping like a baby giraffe!" Brack proclaimed, causing the three of us to roar at the running style.

"Dear God, when are you gonna come up with some new jokes?" Andy ripped on Brack, although he still chuckled at it.

Brack's reply was to continue to clean up the items on the current checklist, visually and verbally verified by both of us, even though we both had the entire list memorized, completed, and checked already.

The efficiency of our crew got us off the ground in mere minutes, with the itemized steps being announced by Brack, "Checklist complete...you suck."

This might've seemed backwards to some. We might've even given the impression that us officers had lost control of the crew if anyone heard the remarks from the back-enders (one of the many nicknames we used for the Flight Engineer and gunner because they sit, well, in the back). But that couldn't have been further from the truth. There were specific reasons why we operated this way.

The four of us in our crew had developed trust and an understanding for one another during the hundreds of missions we'd flown together. We weren't disrespectful, we were family.

As an added bonus, the familial ties we developed assured our Flight Engineer and gunner that us pilots had their backs. If I was on the controls of a .50 caliber on the largest target in this hellhole, I'd want trust from my officers too.

This kind of atmosphere kept everyone loose and relaxed. Besides, if you were so uptight you couldn't take some joking over the intercom or were so incompetent that you couldn't run checklists, handle comms, and mess around at the same time, then you had no business flying combat rescue missions in the worst place on earth.

Our Area of Responsibility or AOR (the geographic region in which we flew every medical evacuation, medevac, mission) was seemingly designed to kill us. From the river village of Marjah in the south to the isolated Musa Qaleh in the north, everyone and everything wanted us dead. We were told insurgents from all over the world had traveled here to join the cause.

Since early 2010, the Marines had slowly been pushing up the Helmand River Valley following their offensive into Marjah.

For years, the British had held the same territory in a tumultuous way. The simple truth, however, was the Brits didn't have the manpower to hold such a massive and hostile region. When the cultural mindset had been dedicated to repelling invaders for thousands of years, I wasn't sure we'd brought enough U.S. Marines to do the job, either. Considering how busy we were, there wasn't much evidence to the contrary.

The particular operation we were supporting had been ongoing for three days. The Marines and a small group of embedded ISAF troops (our allies) had been driving north along the Helmand River and had begun their final phase to encircle a village on the west side of the river.

Shortly after hopping in and strapping her harness on, Dee took the flight controls for the mission, while I ran comms, navigation, and coordinated all the myriad split-second decisions required on a reactive mission such as this. Our flight duties had no complex method of being divided other than taking turns every mission. One of us flew the aircraft while the other ran the show.

Meanwhile, our Pararescue team had completed its weapons and gear setup and finished preparations by clipping their customized rappel harnesses into the helicopter cabin with a single carabiner. The team included one Combat Rescue Officer (CRO) and two Pararescuemen or Para-Jumpers, PJs for short. PJs are highly trained operators that specialize in small team tactics and have been medically trained to a Paramedic level. They operated as a team, or could be integrated with other teams throughout the special operations community. Two more PJs were doing the same routine in the back of PEDRO 24, our wingman.

I smiled as I coordinated our takeoff through the Camp Bastion Tower, which was manned by the hottest-sounding British women (and therefore the highlight of every takeoff). Next, I swapped my radio switch to our Tactical Operations Center (TOC) frequency, callsign MOM, having heard the ready calls from our PJ Team Lead and wingman.

"PEDRO 23 Flight, ready for MIST." I notified our operations staff at MOM that both aircraft were standing by to receive mission and patient specifics.

I hated this part of our missions with a passion. I was a pilot, not a doctor (no pun intended), but the recurrence of violence had forced me to develop a good understanding of trauma care and its associated language. MIST is an acronym that stands for Mechanism, Injury, Signs, and Treatment, which is an assessment of what has occurred, what injury or wound resulted, how the circulation and breathing are, and what has been done to treat the patient.

In reality, however, MIST meant how important the patient was in relation to our aircraft. It meant having to hear over and over, *Gun shot...sucking chest wound...IED blast injury...vitals crashing...* It indicated whether we might be headed into a life-or-death mission, with the threat being not just to the patient's life but also my crew and our team.

There was a human quality that could not be quantified, yet must be accounted for, on these types of sorties, or flights. This instinct, emotion, nature, or whatever it was drove us all to push in a little faster and to take more risks when another person's life was hanging in the balance.

MOM responded immediately, "MIST as follows: blast injury, crushed pelvis, crushed left femur, left ankle fracture, heart rate..."

Suddenly, the other four radios I was manning joined in all at once, led by Bastion Tower's heavily accented voice, "PEDRO 23 Flight, cleared for takeoff..."

Dee cut in halfway through Tower's take-off clearance aggressively, "Power's in."

The engines screamed in tune to the demand while our crew's favorite aircraft, tail #204, heaved us into the sky with her assertive yet smooth power pull. Our wingman, PEDRO 24, took off slightly behind and to the right of us, speaking on a separate radio dedicated solely to our formation.

A simple, "24 copies all," let us know they were in position with a good aircraft and had all the information passed through MOM and Bastion Tower.

"Cleared up and right." Brack was next on the intercom, confirming we weren't headed into anything that would kill us on his side.

Andy stepped in next, visually and verbally verifying our left side was clear, stating, "Left."

I repeated our clearance to Tower, and turned my radio back to the intercom, briefing the crew on our 26-minute ETA, estimated time of arrival. Andy relayed this last part to our staff at MOM on SATCOM, our satellite communications radio, "PEDRO copies MIST, ETA two-six mikes."

No accent this time as he meticulously spelled out each phonetic letter, number, and substituted words such as *mikes* for *minutes*. These little things combined to make a huge difference in minimizing miscommunications.

All five radios and the intercom blared in rhythm and beat to the others, seemingly part of a choreographed musical production. Our operations staff at MOM relayed the MIST to us, the

British controllers in the Tower approved our take-off, called out other traffic, and gave us follow-on instructions.

Dee flew our take-off while Brack and Andy cleared the area and began preparing their .50 caliber side-mounted weapons. Teams and crews coordinated the updated MIST to each other, while I relayed all information and plans passing in and out of our formation.

This exact sequence had been going on for months, and every action we had just taken pointed to a distinct and singular purpose: our patient's life is now the one reason for being here. No matter who or what might get in the way, we will get him, her, or them out.

This isn't to brag, it is simply a statement of who we were and how we operated. We didn't tolerate anyone in our rescue community who didn't feel this way. The mission, our crew, the formation, and the patient were all that mattered. *Fuck my life* was not an expression, it was a cultural mindset.

I completed the final checklist, arming the weapons by flipping the power switch to the .50 calibers in our left turn-out north, beyond the base fences. Now it was time to get down to the nitty gritty. *What the hell are we doing?*

I pulled out the Smart-pack for the operation, a collection of pages loosely glued together that provided a quick reference to callsigns, frequencies, and a detailed GRG (a grid map on which the buildings were numbered for quick response). Flipping the radio to the FIRES frequency, the name for the main tactical channel of any operation, the engines groaned as Dee demanded more power yet again. I took advantage of the few quiet minutes of transit time and familiarized myself with the GRG, trying to assimilate as much of the picture as possible.

A pair of air-to-ground Air Force attack fighters, A-10s, call-sign HAWG, and a pair of Marine helicopter gunships, callsign DEALER, actively prosecuted targets to the north and northeast of our patient. The radio frequency was jam-packed, but we were hearing no communications from the JTAC, or Joint Tactical Air Controller, an airman who embeds with ground units to control air support.

Not hearing the JTAC with FIRES so busy meant one thing — we had no direct line-of-sight to the radio operator. This would require an extra relay for all information to and from us until our reception was no longer blocked by terrain, but I couldn't see any further complications beyond that.

We had been told to standby the first time I tried checking in while enroute. We were only a few miles away from the area at this point, but considering how busy FIRES still was, I held my tongue and instead asked for information from our PJ team about the wounded. The patient and his vitals were reported as stable, but to be honest, a crushed femur was not at the top of our frequent injuries list.

"It's up to the medic...if they move him around and that leg isn't secure, those bone shards can be razor blades all around the femoral artery, bro." Our Team Lead (the most experienced PJ), known as Senior, laid out the scenario so matter-of-factly he could've been describing a recipe for toast.

Dee's response was an immediate left turn to set us up into a 100-foot orbit west of the Green Zone. Her turn into our holding pattern was an acknowledgement to me that she'd heard everything and knew what to do. This saved us from having to speak at all, which was crucial right then.

Typically rescue had priority over any other ongoing action, but when the patient was stable, we sometimes needed to wait. At that moment, we could only hear half of the radio calls. Comms could be such a delicate situation that if you did not jump in at the right time, things could get dangerous in a hurry.

The Helmand River Valley was a massive spread of farmland and compounds a quarter of a mile to more than several miles in width from the edge of the river to the desert border. Beyond that was nothing but monotone sand and mountains in every direction. Our orbit on the western desert side of the river valley put us on the other side of a rocky cliff wall, leaving us terrain-masked, or blocked with no line-of-sight to the JTAC. When an opening in comms finally hit, I had to improvise.

"DEALER, PEDRO," I called on the encrypted frequency.

"PEDRO, go for DEALER," a Marine in the lead helicopter answered.

"PEDRO'S got negative communication with the JTAC. Meet us on 123.9 (alternate frequency) for relay check-in and MIST update." I passed our private frequency to DEALER so we wouldn't jam the FIRES radio.

The next few minutes were a blur of radios and coordination as DEALER outlined the current situation. The wonderful thing about a tactical environment is how real everyone is to each other. Neither before combat nor after have I ever experienced such an amazing coordination of effort in such little time. Nobody cares about drama, and others don't take offense to your tone or facial expression if something isn't asked politely enough. (This makes normal life frustrating as hell for Veterans, but that is another story altogether.)

Time caught up to us as everything until then consisted of daily repetition. DEALER sent the updated MIST along with a situation report (SITREP), and I had zero time after he finished before responding with our entire game plan.

To sum it all up, we were going to monitor patient vital signs while DEALER and HAWG conducted multiple attack runs, and I'd advise when inbound for pickup. Our aircraft would come single ship from the southwest, while our wingman, PEDRO 24, would hold position over the desert.

During this time, DEALER was to remain overhead in its gun pattern at 2,000 feet throughout the pickup as our gunship/ cover aircraft. (A gun pattern is simply an overhead orbit that aircraft fly while conducting air/ground attack runs. The shape is generally desired to follow a racetrack pattern but is designed for a pilot/crew to maximize use of the weapons while considering many other factors, such as collateral risks to friendly ground forces, or friendlies.)

After spelling out those intentions to DEALER, I waited until hearing the repeated relay to the JTAC before turning to Dee. "You cool with that?"

"Oh, God, yeah." Dee chortled.

I passed the GRG map to Brack and Andy. The patient was stable at the moment, so we held this circular flight pattern until the right time.

"I want them to have nothing to do with covering us." Dee enunciated her approval regarding the single-ship part of my plan.

The crew formerly known as our wingman, until the last week, had just swapped back to Khandahar and a new crew had replaced them. The four of us had become close with the previous crew, and we shared a lot of the same philosophies about combat flying. All of us were from the same squadron in Las Vegas and had gone through the last tour in Iraq together. We'd lived, flown, and fought the last five months together. To say the least, we were tight.

Nothing against the new PEDRO 24 crew, but they hadn't yet earned our trust. Not enough to make me turn down a Marine gunship combo overhead, anyway.

As I monitored the FIRES frequency, I understood the situation on the ground had started to deteriorate, as more air-to-ground gun runs from both HAWG and DEALER hadn't seemed to help.

"Hey, we gotta get in there if they have to move him." Senior spoke up, showing both his awareness for the ground situation and how concerned he was for the patient's leg, considering those bone fragments.

"No worries, you make the call," I answered.

I then outlined for the team in detail how we were going to come in low from the southwest, putting the threats to our 10 o'clock, with the patient off to the right. The patient was ready for pickup, but the LZ was still taking fire from the insurgents north and northeast of the compound behind which the JTAC and the Marines prepping our LZ were in cover. We couldn't hear the JTAC, but the communications from HAWG and DEALER revealed how intense it was on the ground.

*Fuck, Senior's right. And they're not going to wait, they're going to move the LZ south after these gun runs.* I grabbed the map I'd been using to point out targets to both Brack and Andy, an extravagance of awareness seldom seen in the dynamic rescue environment. After seeing the few likely options for an alternative LZ, I settled my nerves and waited.

The next couple of minutes seemed to drag by. A small battle raged two miles from us on the other side of the ridge, but we could do nothing until the right moment. Trying to land in the middle of the fight at the wrong time would put the Marine unit at risk for more casualties. The last thing they needed was to deal with us before they were ready. Anxiety set in as we each audibly sifted through the comms for those transmissions relevant to us.

The Afghani desert, hot, blinding, desolate, sat below us as we burned holes in the sky. There's no feeling more helpless than having to sit in a holding pattern, waiting your turn. The entire delay was short, maybe 15 minutes, but when you know what's waiting on the other side...

DEALER unknowingly set off our cue with a simple message. "PEDRO, DEALER relaying updated MIST."

"Send it, DEALER," I called back.

"Blood pressure, 70 over 45..." DEALER began.

"Pilot, we gotta get in there." Senior caught the information about the patient's rapidly lowering blood pressure.

Dee answered by throwing us horizontal into an opposite, hard right turn as she split us single ship from our wingman, ordering them to remain over the desert with a single directive. "PEDRO 23 is stripping."

The barrage of radio traffic intensified for the next minute as her maneuver freed me up to coordinate our inbound approach. The additional strain from the heavily banked turn increased the G-force and pulled each of us into our seats, forcing us to expend a much greater effort to keep our eyes forward.

I looked straight up through the greenhouse glass (the green tinted window above my seat) at the horizon as I copied DEALER'S next transmission. The LZ had moved one compound south, exactly as Senior had predicted.

"PEDRO is two mikes out, 500 feet and below, request DEALER remain in the overhead gun pattern, 500 feet and above." I answered, taking control of the airspace into the LZ.

Cross-checking the instruments and the navigation system for time again as we followed the terrain up a small valley to the ridgeline, our favorite PaveHawk was doing everything asked of her and more, pushing more than 130 mph at 100 feet above the terrain.

The rolling desert hills rose up to meet us, then swept above in a deception of isolation, hiding what waited in the Green Zone for us. We had almost a full minute of flying over countless compounds before hitting the LZ.

Unfortunately, we were all too familiar with this stretch, as it was a mere few miles south of where our sister ship, PEDRO 66, had gone down in June of 2010. A mile closer DEALER'S unit had lost a Cobra attack helicopter in late August. To put it plainly, I loathed this shithole of endless death.

Just before we got to the edge of the valley, I announced our final position over the FIRES frequency before the upcoming approach, "PEDRO is one mike out. Pop smoke, pop smoke, pop smoke." (*Pop smoke* meaning to set off a smoke grenade, so our crew could rapidly identify the landing zone and necessary approach further out.)

DEALER relayed this message to the JTAC, and I expected that to be my last transmission until after the pickup. Now was the perfect time to practice that age-old pilot wisdom of shutting up.

The horizon swung vertical as Dee slammed down the collective and rocked the stick left, executing a maneuver known as a bunt. Immediately leveling the aircraft as our helicopter fell with the sharp cliff that jutted out of the valley's western edge, she'd used our energy and gravity to pull us down the 200-foot wall toward the ground. The helicopter shook from its excessive velocity as she wrenched the collective back into maximum torque, or power, and we rounded out the bottom of the descent into the valley for the approach.

My hands instinctively followed the controls in the event anything unexpected happened. Dee was a great pilot, but as we dropped to tree-top level, there would be no time to recover the helicopter if she was hit.

The immediate rush and seeming near-death intensity of the bunt was more of a necessity than anything else. It minimized our flight profile (how much we stood out) to the insurgents by keeping us as close as possible to the terrain, which decreased the enemies' time to prepare for our landing.

To our PJ customers in the back, it came off as more of an annoyance than anything else, unless they'd been bored lately. If they were bored, they loved this shit.

Glancing back, I saw the PJs screwing off and slapping each other on the back, as they enjoyed the world's fiercest three-dimensional roller coaster. *I guess today's been slow?*

Two seconds later, the environment transformed in stark contrast to the desert calm. Compound after compound, set inside the deep green of marijuana crops and short desert trees, blurred past us. The vibration of the aircraft reaching its maximum speed turned into extreme buffeting. Never satisfied, Dee coaxed every single ounce of torque and knot of speed out of the helicopter in a constant dance on the controls.

White flags zipped past, hung in open display of Taliban support at virtually every compound. The anxiety of the situation was not abnormal, but something else just didn't feel right.

*Fuck, fuck, fuck!...It's too quiet...* I searched for where the LZ should be.

That nagging pull in the back of my mind suddenly exploded into realization: the JTAC hadn't set off a smoke grenade yet, which was critical when landing in a hot LZ.

"PEDRO'S inbound! Pop smoke! Pop smoke! Pop smoke!" I yelled into the encrypted channel.

"Searching!" Andy acknowledged my warning to the crew.

The doors were not attached to the cockpit, but that didn't seem to help as both of us pilots strained and fought against our locked harnesses, trying in vain to see anything at all.

Ironically, some of the greatest minds in human history have devoted their entire lives to seeking ways to define eternity. Hang out 50 feet above the Helmand River Valley Green Zone for 1.37 seconds too long, and trust me, you'll know exactly what the fuck eternity means.

"Contact LZ, 10 o'clock, 500 meters, start your approach!" My right boot stomped the floor intercom switch hard enough to puncture the sheet metal.

The clearances from Andy and Brack came through while the barrel of Andy's .50 caliber cannon swung up to my door. My hands guarded the flight controls, again out of habit and again for no purpose. Dee's approach couldn't have been more perfectly aggressive as she bottomed out the collective, mashed the pedals, and threw us sideways. Shedding massive energy and adjusting the originally-planned straight-in southwestern approach, we slid into an arced approach from the south-southeast.

"PEDRO'S contact red smoke." I offered the JTAC another chance to wave us off if his smoke didn't match the color I called.

Sometimes, an insurgent also popped a smoke grenade, which was an anti-helicopter tactic straight out of the Vietnam playbook. In an unprepared environment, it could sometimes add just enough confusion to get a crew to land to the enemy. This was not a common strategy in this theater, but there were enough reports that it had become a valid threat.

For those unfamiliar with helicopter approaches, please think of a speedboat, approaching perpendicular in relation to a dock. A helicopter approach to an LZ is much like that speedboat coming to the dock at full throttle and simultaneously throwing the wheel full left or right, throttling to full reverse, and stopping the boat parallel to the dock as close as possible without touching it.

Take that, make it three dimensional, immensely more complicated, and include a habitual application of equations in motion. Add in the fact that people you love more than yourself could die if you screwed up, and, lastly, toss in the randomness of brown-outs (a phenomenon where sand and dirt are kicked up by the rotor downwash, which eliminates most-to-all visibility for the last 10 to 80 feet, usually with minimal warning). You now have an education about how much helicopter approaches can suck.

Fast-forwarding back to where I was guiding Dee's approach until she could get her eyes on the smoke, our 3D dock rapidly passed through the 11 o'clock as she rolled us out onto a direct heading. The maneuver had put us in a position where we could land now and talk later. It had also highlighted the hell out of us and put us in a bad spot in which to be low and slow.

I confirmed our pre-landing checks were complete, but before any approach-to-landing calls could be made a shot rang out, then more.

*Crack! Pop! Pop!*

"Go around!" someone yelled into the intercom.

*Pop! Pop! Pop!*

"Go around! Go around!" Brack screamed this time.

*Pop! Pop! Pop!*

The gunfire started so sporadically in the first couple of seconds that it hid our enemies' full capability.

"PEDRO is on the go. Taking fire 100 meters north. Request immediate support!" I cried into the radio.

*Crack! Pop! Crack!*

Dee threw the cyclic forward and ripped the engines into maximum torque as I called out our go-around and request for gunship fire. Opposing gunshots came heavier and heavier from our right. It sounded like being on the wrong end of a firing range with every single weapon on full-automatic pointed straight at us.

However, in spite of everything coming at us, it was eerily quiet. Why weren't we shooting?

*Brack!* I jerked my head back to see his .50 caliber silent.

Enemy .762 rounds poured forth, soon matched in intensity by supporting Marine fire. But Brack was slumped forward, not moving, not shooting.

A horrible thought hit me. *Brack's dead!*

I had a notion that we were probably all dead at that moment, but for some reason it didn't matter. Perhaps only a handful of seconds passed, but each one felt as if it lasted a lifetime.

Suddenly our Flight Engineer moved, alive, and awakened me out of my strange daze. I found I'd twisted my shoulders around and tried screaming his name over the noise of the engines and gunfire, not thinking or bothering to press either intercom mic switch. Unfortunately, there was no time to discuss or get any closure from that vision.

Dee already had us flying more than 100 knots at 20 feet while the JTAC cycled in HAWG and DEALER on alternating gun runs as the Marines' fire responded. He confirmed my request for a patient MIST update after the Marines moved southeast to the next compound.

In response, I requested two more attack runs from both HAWG and DEALER to buy time to transition east of the river and then approach from the southeast, covered by the new compound.

We re-joined with PEDRO 24 and completed the Battle Damage Assessment (BDA), which was our way of directing our wingman to check us for holes.

"Yeah, I had nothing on that last one. I couldn't see shit but rounds coming at us," Brack announced on the intercom.

"No worries, dude," Dee replied, as we all understood.

Daytime positive identification (PID) was sometimes next to impossible, as insurgents knew how to hide pretty damn well. The problem was, women and children hid, too. Nobody wanted to live with killing them by mistake.

No one else said anything. Off our left side, the A-10s dove through thousands of feet on their attack runs while we crossed the Helmand River in complete silence. None of us could believe we were still flying.

We set up in a quick holding pattern two minutes from the new LZ and waited again with our wingman over the desert. Within one turn, the JTAC was ready and cleared us back in, confirming we were comfortable with the attack runs continuing until right before we landed. Trying not to laugh too hard, I let him know in not-so-many-words that we did not mind the fire support on final approach.

Dee dove down the eastern bank of the Helmand River and leveled us out 50 feet above the water, maximum airspeed announcing itself again through an intense shaking of our Pave-Hawk as we demanded more than ever intended by any Sikorsky engineer.

"PEDRO'S one mike out. Pop smoke! Pop smoke! Pop smoke!" I asserted this loud and clear.

HAWG immediately replied to my transmission, dropping perpendicular from thousands of feet up, descending with a vengeance on the targets north of our LZ. A second later, it seemed as if the entire northern half of the village went up in a mushroom fireball, rising hundreds of feet into the air.

"Fuck, yeah!" Andy marveled at the spectacle.

In contrast to minutes earlier, this landing was smooth, maybe one of the calmest approaches we had ever had. In less than 60 seconds, we were airborne again with the patient, passing his vitals and our ETA to operations at MOM.

Compounds slid past us as the PJs in the back worked over the wounded. In spite of everything going on around us, a heavy quiet overtook the aircraft, as all onboard attempted to create the most audibly sterilized environment possible. Meanwhile, the makeshift surgeon's table a few feet behind me in the cabin became anything but silent as our team worked to stabilize and secure our patient.

Two minutes after takeoff, we re-joined with PEDRO 24, heading south toward Camp Bastion as we climbed up to 2,000 feet.

*Navigation system's up, comms up...* I made a subconscious effort to ignore everything behind me. I'd already completed my non-flying checklists without thought, but my mind was still trying to figure out the next problem.

Unable to sit still, I kicked my leg up on the empty doorframe and stared off into the endless desert. Pff, pff, pff. Tiny clouds of dust snapped off of the leg of my pants as I flicked them.

The next 20 minutes felt more like 20 hours. All of the timing, patient status, and aircraft radio calls were made, but to be honest, I was going through the motions. More like a robot than anything else, I don't remember dropping the patient off, re-fueling, or landing.

Pausing after climbing out of the cockpit, I watched our maintenance dudes laugh alongside Brack as he shook his head in disbelief that we hadn't been hit. I didn't have the awareness to even search for our head crew chief, but I don't think I saw her.

Not too long before, she'd confided in me her need to go behind the aircraft hangar and cry almost every time we got into a firefight. "I can't stand the look on your faces...and the ones who don't come back..."

Instead, I stood next to Andy for a few minutes, sharing in a well-earned victory chew. As a good officer, concerned for the health and wellbeing of his staff sergeant, I'd helped Andy quit smoking...by switching to chewing tobacco. We now celebrated living after each mission with a victory chew.

Disgusting? Maybe, but it wasn't like we could stroll down to the local pub. We expected to be called back out at any second, and that lesson had been reinforced hundreds of times. I half-expected that any minute now the next *Scramble* to interrupt our moment of peace would result in one of us going postal. No kidding, this time meant that much.

Dust hung heavy in the air as we stood there, not speaking, not even looking at each other. I'd gotten to the point where I was uncomfortable not having him next to me. If I'd known this was to be my last mission ever, I might've paid better attention.

I'd flown hundreds of combat rescue missions over Iraq and Afghanistan and would never return to either, yet for me, the war was just beginning...

# CHAPTER 3

# THREATS ALL AROUND

## EAST COAST, UNITED STATES, FALL, 2010

*Why are all these people staring at me?* Walking through the busy Philadelphia airport on the way home from Afghanistan felt more like trying to find my way through a maze built of aggressive strangers.

*There are so many...* My mind attempted to calm things down rationally but was powerless to turn off that overwhelming feeling of despair. I wasn't able to even appreciate the irony that I could probably fly any plane here, but I couldn't locate a simple gate because of the endless number of people!

Passive-aggressively, my brain started searching for things wrong with everyone around me. I felt as if they were surrounding, trapping, and suffocating me. I was shocked by how many there were, not having seen more than a dozen or so people at once in months. Not too long into my hunt for the gate I had to stop and find a quiet place to hide.

One thing that struck me about coming home was seeing how obese we'd become as a nation. I had forgotten this particular aspect of American life. As I found a seat away from the crowd, my thoughts swung to hating people for what was obviously wrong with them, which, in this case, was their weight.

It wasn't that our country's health crisis had happened overnight during my deployment. My judgment had been reshaped after spending most of the year surrounded by some of the fittest people on the planet.

I'd long ago learned the lesson that staying in shape not only helped pass the time, it was vital. Teams, and their operators, wouldn't trust anyone who let themselves go. This also applied to aircrew.

I was apparently using this same logic as an excuse to label others in the midst of my own anxiety. It was a way of looking for an external reason to explain this internal discord.

The heaviest person I'd seen in months, appearing to be in his late 30s, and long overdue on his next heart stoppage, somehow managed to squeeze himself into a seat across from me.

*Really?* Multiple empty sections of seats, next to another almost deserted gate... *Sure, plop down next to me. It's cool. I don't mind.*

He could've legitimately been at the right place for his next flight, but I was too bothered by my own emotions to consider common sense. Instead, my mind reeled with resentment while the revulsion built.

The dude sucked down a foot-long chili cheese dog while his middle-school-aged son gobbled up an even larger Philly cheese steak sandwich next to him. Unable to stand the sight any longer, I stalked away to find an emptier area.

I moved from section to section, as nobody seemed to notice I wanted to be left alone. *What is their problem?*

Wedging myself in the back corner at an unused gate, I felt comfortable I would finally be left to myself when the jetway door itself slammed open less than three feet away. *Holy fuck!*

Two airport workers strutted out, unaware of how much they had pissed me off. Gathering my gear, I wondered for the first time where an angry gunner was when you needed one.

*Damn it, Andy, how many times have I told you we got your back?* My mood changed as I recalled how it had taken a couple of weeks before our gunner felt we trusted his decisions.

*In his defense, Andy hasn't had a great history with gringos.* The dialogue played in my head like my own personal film.

*That's below the belt!* My conscience shouted from wherever it hid.

The smile on my face probably made me appear ridiculous, but I didn't care. The memory of my brother put me in a better mood than any one of these unknown, over-privileged, pampered people ever could.

A realization that I'd inadvertently drifted to a food court penetrated my pessimistic thoughts. *Burgers, fries, cookies, and carbonated paint thinner to wash it down with. Could someone please sell actual food?*

I decided I'd rather be hungry than join the unconscious herd that either shuffled toward, or was already in the process of, strapping on their own personal feed bags.

*No wonder everyone in the entire world hates people in the United States.* My thoughts continued down the path of despising all those around me. The ironic part of this situation was that I'd been overweight in the past as well. However, that didn't matter one bit as my mind sought a reason for this misery. I needed something or someone to blame for how bad I felt inside.

Somehow, in my endless wandering I managed to find my gate, but that did nothing to improve my attitude. Every single one of the hundreds, perhaps thousands, of people I saw seemed miserable.

I recalled random things I'd read online in an effort to justify the vile taste in my mouth. Comments posted to various online news reports I'd read in my down time popped into my mind.

*Why do they whine about that place? They've got it easy.* One blogger had commented on a story from COP Nolen, a location in Afghanistan I couldn't erase from my memory. Shared perspectives from the infantile minds of sissies who would never take part in combat made my blood boil.

*Which one of you wrote that?* I screamed inside myself, as if I could actually find a handful of unidentifiable individuals amongst millions. My body shook from the anger, and tears filled my eyes with the memories of the wounded. The immature judgment I couldn't get out of my head made me feel like an enemy to every single person there.

*Seriously, where is my crew?* Even Dee's hippy-ish approach to life would have had me rolling as I imagined her thoughts about these tall babies surrounding me. She certainly had a handle on how to treat others with respect, but no way could she have hidden her disgust.

For no reason whatsoever, I abhorred them all. To the core of my being, I felt a deep hatred toward everyone around me as I slid down to the floor against another meaningless wall in this trap of noise and cleanliness. I wanted to drop each of them into the Arghandab River Valley in Afghanistan and leave them for dead.

*Sounds pretty good!* Andy's embellished Mexican-American accent re-playing in my head calmed my breathing as I realized my body shook from the thoughts of those days.

*Yeah, well, don't fuck with my patients.* I had no clue this happened, but my mind was already translating the suppressed pain into secondary emotions, mostly anger.

This hostility caused my brain to search constantly for the cause. In this case, I was fixated on finding anyone who had bad-mouthed the 101st Airborne's Artillery Company at COP Nolen.

*Five in one day, eleven the next... From one damn company...* The tears welled up, overfilled capacity and trickled down my face while the memories crept in.

As the line to board my commercial airline formed nearby, I internally gathered myself up and leaned against the window, waiting until the last minute before jumping into the crowd. Noticing a shorter, brown-haired lady's judgment, I averted my eyes and looked outside. *Hate you, too.*

Almost time to board, I attempted to calm myself down, succeeding moderately as I shuffled with the line toward the ramp. The feeling from earlier was so powerful that I could still taste it. Somehow, I made it all the way to my seat before the anxiety of not being busy disrupted my thoughts once again.

The pilot's voice talking overhead sent my mind reeling in discomfort. Thoughts of COP Nolen and the 101st's Artillery Company deployed there started to creep in.

*You can slow it back, Pilot.* The memory spoke out of nowhere.

The first time I heard that call from my pararescue friend rang as loudly as it had just then sitting in the airline passenger seat. We'd been flying back to Khandahar racing to drop off our last patient from COP Nolen, when I heard this. The PJ Team

Lead had meant one thing, our patient was VSA (Vital Signs Absent), and I should save the engines for the next mission.

My body shook as I tried not to think of what happened next. The trembling and tears gave me an excuse to slide over to the empty spot next to the window and plan how to choke the yuppie in the aisle seat, should he ask why I was crying.

*Fuck you, that's why.* One of my favorite responses came to mind.

Having some manner of isolation in a different seat allowed my mind to settle, but it kept settling on that day. *That horrible day.*

*"You can slow it back,"* was not the only call. My mind pointed out.

*What the hell is going on with me?* These thoughts were welling up too close to the surface.

I pulled a water bottle out of my lone carry-on bag, trying to center myself. I couldn't fathom being stuck next to anyone right then, and I felt more assurance that I'd be left alone as the seconds ticked by. Instead of being relieved by the increasing odds of isolation, more anxious thoughts of my crew and how the hell I'd ended up here volleyed through my head.

Finally, the airline baggage employees loaded the last cart of luggage onto the plane, and all of the passengers felt the reverse pull as we were towed from parking to the taxiway.

*Clear back and left...right,* memories of our helicopter taxi calls mingled with the aircraft's present backward motion and sent my tired mind reeling from the polar opposite situations.

Within moments, I'd be consumed by what was clawing its way up from the mental depths...

\* \* \*

*Without a clue as to why, I'd become hateful toward every-one around me. I didn't even know how to question where this emotion came from. In retrospect, I was creating reasons for my feelings by judging others, because it was easier than deal-ing with my own energy.*

*Had I known how to examine myself, the intrusive thoughts might've led me to a different path, one that would have allowed me to re-define my conceptual changes post-combat. However, the focus on the events themselves was far easier to deal with than sitting still in the present emotions, once again taking me back to Afghanistan, 2010.*

## KHANDAHAR AFGHANISTAN, SUMMER, 2010

"That motherfucker's got a phone." Andy pointed out with his .50 caliber.

A quick glance out my door, down the barrel to where he was aimed, confirmed it. A random military-age-male, miles from any road, was standing on top of a lone mountain peak holding a satellite phone to his ear.

"Cleared hot." I grinned approval to open fire as I caught view.

For the second time that day, we were on our way into the Arghandab River Valley, heading to an LZ just outside of COP Nolen. I was leading our helicopter formation, PEDRO 55 Flight, just past the mountain climber. His pinnacle was part of the first of two perpendicular ridge lines. The second marked the river valley, the Green Zone. We would be holding 2,000 feet of alti-tude, theoretically keeping us clear of small-arms fire, until cross-ing the second mountain ridge and descending past the river.

41

I was partly joking about killing that guy, yet seriously didn't care what Andy did at the same time. We all knew his purpose, and it wasn't as a telemarketer.

It was still early morning, so the man had either climbed in the dark or slept there. No one in Afghanistan except the wealthy or well-backed had a phone. We were at least 10 miles from the nearest compound or dirt road, and no dudes in this area took sat-phones on spirit-hikes. All of this pointed to only one reason for this guy being where he was, and technically, per our rules of engagement, one correct action on our part.

Silently, I cussed myself out in response for dropping yaw (stream-line, or, left/right tail alignment) out of my vision. I corrected the tail rotor with a touch more pressure from my left foot and focused more on my crosscheck, how quickly I bounced my eyes from one gauge to the next.

Our airspeed had suffered a half-knot consequence, but I had no more power to pull from the collective and was trying to keep us above 120 knots (130 to 140 mph). The tension that comes with any mission is always amped up when a Cat Alpha (Category Alpha or urgent surgical) patient's life is on the line.

The list of things that make you anxious as a helicopter pilot far exceed the 30,000 moving parts keeping you airborne. Any young pilot wanting to become an old pilot never stops scanning the environment for hazards, the instruments and gauges for hazards, planning the future to avoid hazards, and is always thinking of where to land when any hazard becomes too real.

What nobody had explained to my younger self as a flight student was rescue pilots didn't have the luxury of consciously focusing on safety. There was too much going on to allow for *what if* thoughts. In between constant analysis, planning, coordination, and everything else, even the thought of safety was an indulgence helicopter pilots could ill afford. You either know what to do in those moments before you step to the aircraft or you don't.

"I totally should've killed him." Andy continued, expressing his regret as the next range of desert mountains fell behind us.

He was right, that dude was there to call descriptions and numbers of aircraft to other insurgents so they could spend the day blowing up Americans and target us when we went in to rescue the wounded. I felt the same regret. We should've killed him.

The section of the valley we were heading to was controlled by FOB Terra Nova. Terra Nova was the main Forward Operating Base a couple miles north of the Arghandab River, which commanded and supported its smaller Combat Outposts (COPs). COP Nolen was directly south and the farthest eastern outpost on this section of the river. Insurgents were putting up heavy resistance to the recent U.S. troop surges, particularly in this valley, and had obviously used the dust storm of the previous days to litter the fields with Improvised Explosive Devices (IEDs), mines or buried bombs.

Everybody was always so silent on missions into contested areas, especially on repeat sorties to the same LZ like this. However, in retrospect, I don't think we noticed. Radios chirped out, patient status updates were requested and sent, but for the most part we all kept our mouths shut and fell into whatever habitual routines kept us sane. On some sorties, the one thing that could save us from going mental was to keep busy.

Insurgents owned the river valley south and west of our target LZ, so crossing the perpendicular mountain range a few miles east of the target area allowed us to descend and approach from the north, the single way we could get in and avoid ground fire. Thanks to the wind, our heavy bird, and the oppressive heat, we couldn't avoid the threat on the way out.

"PEDRO 55 Flight, intel reports insurgents being instructed to target ISAF medevac." A member of our operations staff advised us over SATCOM, the satellite communications radio.

*Yup, we should've killed him.* All members of the crew thought this in unison.

"PEDRO copies." Andy technically answered in a professional way.

But his response barely covered up the fact that he wanted to shove his muzzle in someone's face for irritating him with facts we already knew. Our relaxed position at 2,000 feet hid what was about to happen, but we were under no illusions of safety.

We hadn't finished dropping off the first two Cat Alpha patients when the call for the next five came in. We'd been immediately re-tasked to go pickup two Cat Alphas and three Cat Bravos, which to us meant two urgent surgical patients and three surgical patients.

All seven that day were from the Army's 101st Airborne. The only difference with this medical mission was, the platoon on patrol wasn't close enough to get the wounded back to an established LZ.

This was common here, considering how biblical everything was, with no infrastructure to speak of. As a result, we were minimally instructed to land to a Point of Injury (POI) or an unknown Landing Zone one mile away from the combat outpost.

Everything from small arms to IEDs to rocket propelled grenades (RPGs) were a possibility, and there were no double-stacked barriers set up around a POI, like an established LZ would have. Mentally there was no way to prepare for this pickup, and everything we were about to face would be happening in a helicopter as large as a greyhound bus moving at Nascar speed 50 feet above the ground.

Neither of our aircraft had the power to get all five patients out, so we planned a phased infil (approach), meaning our wingman would land first. We would then land the instant our wingman was airborne with their patients. LONGKNIFE, a pair of Army OH-58s, or Kiowas, were to act as the cover gunships, providing strafing runs with their dual underslung .50 caliber weapons and rocket pods.

Under normal circumstances, this plan would've been tactically risky, more so considering the past two days of dust storms and, of course, our friend with the phone. However, we understood that both Cat Alpha patients were double amputees, and at least one was close to crashing (in the field, an amputee label means a tourniquet has been applied — the patient may/may not still have the full limb but the surgical team will make the final decision). At this point, the choice was already made.

That thought stood out as I led our formation over the last mountain ridge and into the Arghandab River Valley. An unreadable 2,000+ feet became 200 in a heartbeat as the rad-alt (radar altimeter, a digital display of our altitude above the ground) swiftly picked up the rising ridgeline perpendicular to our path.

Anticipating what came next, our wingman's pilot pushed close to abeam us as we dove with the sharply falling terrain. This would keep them from flying behind us, and as a result, over the same threats. This also forced anyone shooting at us to pick one helicopter to target instead of us flying over them in a beeline. Sometimes, dividing the opposing fire in half was the best we could do to mitigate a threat.

The silence of our cockpit suddenly exploded into the calls of battle. Our radios had gained line-of-sight, and we were receiving the FIRES frequency. Our encrypted FM radio shared the cold, familiar voices of LONGKNIFE and the ground commander as we waited our turn to speak.

For the most part our tactics in and around an LZ were pretty simple. We always flew with two aircraft so one could land while the other provided air-ground cover with its dual .50 caliber guns. Our plan for a phased-infil approach meant we would leave our gun pattern/overhead orbit and land while the other aircraft was taking off.

We decided which helicopter landed or flew as the cover ship by the age-old practice of taking turns, like kids. We had picked up the last patients, so now it was our wingman's turn to land. I directed our wingman to push in front of us, allowing them to lead our formation into the LZ area.

Ground rush filled my windscreen as I turned to follow PEDRO 56, rounding out the bottom of our descent. I pulled maximum power, pushing the stick further forward, and closed the separation within our formation.

Dee, meanwhile, had waited long enough and took control of the situation over the FIRES frequency. "LONGKNIFE, PEDRO is two mike out, will remain 500 feet and below, request you maintain above 500 feet, exfil will be west and north."

Her coordination with the Kiowas prosecuting a target could not have sounded more precise, and both callsigns did as she directed. But to us, she sounded stressed, which was how we all felt, doing the same thing again. Sometimes, I hated knowing my crew so well.

FOB Terra Nova seemed quiet as we approached it at 50 feet and more than 120 knots. The rough shaking of aircraft tail #204 as I pushed and maintained her beyond all normal limits made for rough guesses on our old pitot tube instruments. Dropping power out, rolling into a perpendicular bank, I pulled maximum power back in and noticed nothing strange as I glanced up through the greenhouse glass at the FOB. I supposed that the only weird thing was how calm this place appeared compared to what was happening two miles away.

Snapping our roll to vector us into position, I maneuvered us loosely off PEDRO 56's right side for this landing, which was where the threat would most likely hit them from. I also wanted to remain far enough back that I could hit 150 feet to enter the gun pattern when our wingman began the approach.

Dee directed her last call over FIRES frequency. "PEDRO'S one mike out. Pop smoke! Pop smoke! Pop smoke!"

PEDRO 56 continued its path for a matter of seconds then ever so slightly tipped the nose up, indicating the start of their approach into the Landing Zone. The power taken out would have soon become evident with the difference in speed and closure rate between the two aircraft, but I'd already taken the cue.

Halfway through our climb to 150 feet, I de-conflicted our line-of-fires on the threat by climbing above PEDRO 56 before passing. In other words, I put us above their gun barrel while we flew past, so that they wouldn't have to shoot through us. This allowed us to simultaneously enter the gun pattern while our wingman landed to load their patient.

With PEDRO 56 low and slow on short final of their approach, I threw us over left yet again, rolling into a near horizontal bank. Feeling the turn pull us into our seats, I increased Gs to keep it as tight as possible, and ended up at 150 feet and 80 knots, perpendicular to our wingman's landing. Brack's .50 caliber barrel swept the plaid green of the trees, the marijuana, the river, and the farmland off of our right side for threats.

"Can't see shit for this dust today!" our Flight Engineer declared.

Counting down our gun pattern, I waited for the right timing and distance. Despite his estimation on poor visual acuity, I trusted Brack and kept my eyes ahead to where we were going. We knew where the insurgents were, generally speaking, but we couldn't simply target random compounds or farmland on hunches. As such, firing without first being fired upon was not ever a consideration for us. Thankfully, nobody was shooting, although the reasons why were unknown to us.

"Down and left." I notified the crew of our impending departure from this pattern.

Before Andy had uttered the word *Clear*, I banked over hard left and down, away from where we knew the threat to be, pulled maximum power, and descended down to 50 feet for a count of one...two...three. I rolled us over to a right bank and pulled the stick back as much as possible, feeling the aircraft shake hard with the increased G onset.

My hands and feet meanwhile danced a delicate ballet of tightening the turn while climbing back to 150 feet without giving up speed. Pull too hard, we get slow and become an easy target to be shot out of the sky. Pull too soft, we end up flying directly over the enemy and become even easier to shoot. The aggressive turn made for poor reliance on instruments and a need to trust in gut feeling. I loved this part of being a pilot.

*Wiggle those fingers and toes, Lieutenant. Just wiggle those toes...* The memory of my old Vietnam-veteran flight instructors didn't seem so crazy anymore.

Bringing my crosscheck back down from the overhead greenhouse window, the instruments slowly quit shaking as I rolled out on our re-attack. Power, rad-alt, airspeed. Power, rad-alt, airspeed... Everything looked stable.

It was now Andy's turn to sweep the threat. His thumbs guarded the triggers, cannon at bay, begging for someone, anyone, to fuck with him. Our three-man team, their feet and modified M-4 assault rifles hanging out the cabin sides, backed him up for this last pass.

Hearing our wingman call *Down* and having taken no fire, I banked us sharply north to hold within a 30-second response range as now we were the ones exposed and vulnerable.

This was against our published tactics, but it was deliberate in an effort to minimize our formation's profile. Our limitations in not seeing much today made staying overhead in a gun pattern not worth it. Besides, no helicopter should orbit long over any objective, as this could attract every insurgent in the area.

Gunners love to make fun of pilots for our apparent unquenchable thirst to use math to prove things, and this random pattern we flew was no different. I had calculated it earlier at the alert shack, in the midst of Andy's non-stop humor at my expense. To explain it simply, staying between approximately one kilometer outbound and two kilometers inbound kept our aircraft within 30 seconds of being able to engage any threat to our wingman.

Keeping us in and out of the northern edge of the Green Zone in this 30-second response area left us in perfect position to retaliate against any threat, and people in these parts usually left us alone. It would be a lie, however, if I didn't admit the reactions of the locals bothered me.

Women would become terrified and take off, many times on all fours, to their younger children. The kids we were supposed to be helping threw rocks at us, while the old men raised their arms and swatted us away in obvious dislike of us even being there. Despite hearing constantly that insurgents were traveling from outside Afghanistan, we never seemed to see any local males of fighting age.

"From PEDRO 56, we're going to load four patients. Both Alphas are crashing, and two Bravos are ready now. We are 30 seconds to takeoff." Our wingman's pilot warned of their impending departure over our inter-plane radio frequency.

*Thank God.* I never would've admitted it, but the heat, the non-stop patients, the locals' behaviors, and even the dust were getting to me.

Our wingman's transmission needed no response from me, Dee would cover any and all communication necessary from us. I instead acknowledged their call by throwing us over in a hard right bank, brought up maximum power, and fought to keep the nose level while pulling it sharply across the horizon.

Their slight change to load the patient was no huge deal, it would only take a little more power from what was available. Either way their 30-second warning released us to start toward the LZ. Having received no opposition during PEDRO 56's landing, we were continuing with the phased-infil approach and would be landing directly behind their takeoff.

"PEDRO is 30 seconds to phased egress. PEDRO 56 will be taking off with a left turnout north, below 500 feet. PEDRO 55 is inbound from the north, one mike out," Dee responded to our wingman's transmission by relaying our game plan to LONG-KNIFE on the FIRES frequency.

Her call had granted approval of PEDRO 56's plan, told them which direction to take off, and de-conflicted both of us with our cover gunships, LONGKNIFE. It also advised the ground commander of our plan and told me to press in.

The turn to put us in position to land was my way of agreeing with her plan without speaking. Anyone who agreed stayed quiet so that only problems, exceptions, or obstacles to the plan could be heard. We had spent countless hours perfecting all of these little common-sense tricks (that are not so common).

Starting our approach, I could barely make out our wingman's position in the trees due to the intense dust. We would be landing straight behind PEDRO 56's takeoff in an attempt to minimize time in the terminal area as much as possible. Surprisingly, in spite of everything going on, things were proceeding according to plan. As I watched our wingman begin his takeoff, I continued our approach to the near-simultaneous pattern of guidance from my crew.

All too suddenly our wingman went defensive. "PEDRO 56 is taking ground fire from our 5 o'clock, on the go..."

*Shit!* I pulled maximum power, breaking off the approach.

I used our higher energy, positioning, and airspeed to cut the turn to PEDRO 56's outside and right as they were in a slow left break. We passed slightly above and right of our wingman's aircraft as her crew struggled to get more airspeed. Brack was free to fire, yet held, unable to positively identify any insurgents. I checked our aircraft left to fully enter the gun pattern at Andy's direction, confirming our parameters, then swung my eyes out to re-acquire our wingman. Below 50 feet, they were nowhere to be seen.

*Fuck, fuck, fuck!...Where are they?* Frustratingly, I needed to hold our pattern axis for another, 3...2...1...

Breaking off the gun pattern and away from the threat, we began searching for our Chalk 2. Not having visual of PEDRO 56 was not necessarily bad. We only had a quarter mile of visibility, and besides, our aircraft blended too well with the scenery and vegetation, even for us sometimes.

These thoughts were in the back of my mind as we frantically scanned the horizon for our wingman. *Please let them still be...*

Meanwhile, Dee, scanning for other threats in addition to our wingman, was also busy on FIRES coordinating the split-up with LONGKNIFE.

"Left's visual of PEDRO 56, at our 9 o'clock for one mile!" Andy announced.

We all heaved a collective sigh of relief.

Almost simultaneously, PEDRO 56 finally came through the inter-plane frequency, "PEDRO 55, 56 is off your 8 o'clock for 1.5 (miles). Request re-join and BDA."

"PEDRO'S hook right, zero-seven-zero, 56 has the lead," I responded with cheer, giving our wingman the lead and agreeing to do a visual sweep of the helicopter.

"Hey, Brack, call our turn for me." I held off until he had sight of PEDRO 56 passing behind us and tried concentrating on the scenery of the northern desert instead.

"Yeah, I gotcha. Start your turn in 5...3..."

I banked the aircraft hard right at maximum power on the timing of his *1*.

We had a battle damage assessment to get done, so I dove down and tucked us in off the left, then swapped underneath and across to the right. Dee let them know that we saw no holes and, more importantly, that nothing was leaking from the helicopter.

Well, nothing new seemed to be leaking, anyway. With that out of the way, we still had another patient to recover.

"What's your patient status, 56?" Dee inquired over the inter-plane frequency.

I swung our aircraft one last time under and around our wingman to finish the BDA.

"We have to return to base, both Alphas are crashing." PEDRO 56 in no uncertain terms let us know we were on our own.

"Word," Dee replied, although I swear I heard her mind screaming *Shit!*

My response was to silently break us away from our wingman and swing in a northern loop, returning to pick up our last patient.

Technically, we were required to hold and request permission to go in single ship. Some pencil-pusher a thousand miles away was required to confirm whether we were expendable or not on any given day. However, on a personal level, we had each already made the subconscious decision to forget about this before taking off.

Our behavior spoke for itself, *Our aircraft, our patient, our choice.* And we had each already chosen to follow Dee every time.

We pressed in on the only approach that we could, the same that we had begun minutes before PEDRO 56 took fire. We had no choice that day, with the high temperatures and low wind.

Also as before, no insurgent fired at us on the approach, and we found out why on the ground. The LZ had a decent-sized hill off our 11 o'clock, while the platoon held that ground and the surrounding tree lines.

Not knowing which patient this was, able to see he could walk and had a bunch of bandaging on his upper body, I began prepping our takeoff. A quick discussion of power, trees, and which direction to expect the fire to come from was all that was necessary while the team finished securing our patient.

I mentally shut out all sight and sound of the cabin, instead inching in a bit of power. The helicopter, as a result, felt like she was dancing on her toes, chomping at the bit and ready to be unleashed. The door was slammed shut as I ripped in the remaining power, launching us airborne and upward into whatever would meet us.

Mashing the tail around, we had so little power it was as if I had to claw our way forward over the trees. Flying heavy on a hot day took most of the aircraft's free power away, and there was nothing sexy about taking off either with marginal power or with obstacles in front of you. To make matters worse, the threat off our right made time slow to a crawl.

"Tail's clear." Andy called, hanging out the left side.

I pushed the cyclic further forward, dove toward the ground with no power to stop, fire support in the tree line at our tail. Absolutely nothing mattered except ramping up our airspeed.

Insurgents who weren't within range of the 101st's platoon suddenly took this chance to fire at us, as the takeoff had left us exposed.

*Pop! Pop! Pop!*

A three-round burst came at us from the 5 o'clock while our PJs returned fire and Brack swung his .50 caliber aft. One burst was all he had time to fire before the helicopter finally had enough speed for me to act.

True, I could've handled the maneuver a little softer. Our Team Lead almost shot his foot off as I threw the cyclic over so hard that his nearly six-foot frame was tossed against the opposite door. But, like I told him later, at least the shots quit after that.

Pressing north to depart the Green Zone, we were soon up to maximum airspeed at treetop level. Twenty minutes later, entering Khandahar airspace, we were being asked how quickly we could drop the patient, fuel up, and hightail it back to COP Nolen.

* * *

We ran through the motions this time around: navigation system updated, power calculated, and the helicopter cabin set. Being another mission to almost the exact same place, however, we had the sequence memorized. The same airborne unit was still pinned down and had suffered three more casualties in the short time that it took us to drop the previous five off.

This third trip was for a double amputee Category Alpha and two head trauma Category Bravos. Our repeat performance went almost exactly as the previous one had, except that we were able to get all of the patients out on our aircraft and kill one of the insurgents targeting us on the way out.

The climb out over the northern edge of the desert next to the Arghandab River Valley took the same time as the previous missions. Anxiety practically became a fifth crew member with the occasional surgical calls that rang through.

*Please don't let this dude die on us...* I couldn't help the painful thoughts that came up.

*Shit!* I corrected our altitude, which slowed us by two knots of velocity.

It was difficult to fight the urge to descend and pick up speed through this intermediate, desolate valley east-northeast of Khandahar City. I'd done that before and was convinced it was faster to stay up high.

The flight home was almost a solo skill routine, balancing torque, yaw, altitude, and heading in a constant dance to produce the fastest results with a double amputee's life on the line. On top of that, nobody in the crew talked much while there was a patient being attended to.

I'm sure that some people could tune out everything no matter the situation. I am not one of those people, unfortunately. Somehow I started to take personal responsibility with the patient count increasing after each mission.

Finally cresting the southern edge of the valley, I used our descent down the bleak slope to pick up as much speed as possible. Routine pilot thinking, such as the next waypoint, the next event, radio calls, and other options all became advanced algorithms when cries of, *Get another tourniquet on the left first, it's oozing out...all right, he's stuck,* broke intermittently through the intercom.

Khandahar City and its one million residents were a couple of miles off of our right side as we flew south, but it might as well have been on the other side of the planet for how dusty it was. Less than half a mile out we finally made out the stark contrast of pavement known as Highway One. The lonely gas station we'd passed hundreds of times was a testament to the desolate nature of this hellhole, as I do not remember seeing another one anywhere else. Pushing through the last stretch of desert before hitting one of the busiest airfields in the world, Brack and Andy finished their de-arming checklists as we passed Three Mile Mountain.

The radios began to blow up like there was some kind of natural disaster going on, but actually that was just a normal day. Dee took care of coordinating with Air Traffic Control (ATC) and Khandahar Tower while I set us up to land at the hospital's helicopter pad. Thankfully, we had priority over every aircraft with an Alpha patient on board, so we seldom waited to cross the busy airfield.

I set us up on a shallow approach to the hospital pad and pushed it in as quickly as possible. With as much fuel as we had burned off, I could feel the extra power and used all of it, keeping the aircraft as smooth and level as possible for the patient, yet not taking any extra time we didn't have.

In less than 30 seconds, our team of PJs were off with their patient and gear to brief the surgical team, continuing care while we took off and flew across the airfield to the Hot Pits, a large, bunkered area where helicopters could re-fuel while still running.

After landing and hooking up the gas lines, there wasn't much to do for a few minutes but watch the gas gauge climb to the magic number. Andy and Brack each had to stand outside their respective sides of the helicopter, run checklists, and make sure nothing caught fire. It was a great time to make sure we hadn't been shot, but it was an even better time for my favorite game: messing with my gunner.

"Yo, Andy, come over here, man," I called him to my door.

For a while, I'd found a way to joke with him after any tough flight. This time though, he'd at last caught on.

Trying to talk but laughing through the intercom, he finally responded, "Go fuck yourself!"

This sent all four of us into hysterics. Playing around felt good. To be honest, doing anything human after these missions felt great.

Before I could mockingly defend myself, our radio broke through in an all-too-familiar way: "PEDRO, MOM has another mission for you. Advise when ready to copy..."

* * *

Diving with the terrain again, we awaited the upcoming approach, all the while getting closer to our objective. The LZ was different, but the winds, power, temperature, all of it left us with the exact same approach and takeoff options as before. There was only one way in or out.

LONGKNIFE'S pair of OH-58 Kiowa helicopters danced between the valley ridge lines, diving time and again into their gun runs, desperate to suppress the insurgents as we sped closer.

Being PEDRO 56's turn to pick up the patient, we escorted our wingman in the same manner as before...and were immediately shot off of the LZ. Without any identification of the insurgents, I broke us away as a formation and set up over the northern desert while Dee tried to find us a better way in.

This meant that she was bouncing between conversations with the Kiowas and the ground commander, while trying to coordinate approval to land in a hot LZ with staff officers a thousand miles away via SATCOM. Per our rules, we couldn't land in a hot, or contested, Landing Zone without high-level approval. Our issue with this (and the reason we sometimes "delayed" reporting a hot LZ) was how long it took to get through all of the layers.

Minutes later, plan in place, yet no closer to getting the micromanaged approval, Dee made the best decision. "From PEDRO 55, LZ is cold, cancel high risk request," she lied.

She hadn't finished canceling the useless oversight before I had the helicopter near horizontal again, banking inbound at 50 feet. Fighting to keep the airspeed above 110 knots in the turn, I rolled out on the modified approach heading that she'd also just set up with all players over the FIRES frequency.

No longer needing the safety of the ground, I made sure to climb early and slow back, which exposed our crew at 200 feet. This also set up Brack and Andy with a stable firing platform and extra time to see anything coming. The mental dance between being defensive versus aggressive, separated only by the situation and sometimes just mere seconds, was fairly unique to rescue.

Our wingman, on the other hand, had pushed this approach in as fast and as low as possible, taking no fire this time, "PEDRO 56 is wheels down."

Technically, this also made Dee's lie true, for the moment. I broke off and dove back down to 50 feet as fast as possible, getting my crew out of the scariest environment imaginable. After all, we needed to set up to do it all again.

In the middle of arcing toward the battlefield, our situation changed drastically. PEDRO 56, stuck on the ground loading a patient, started taking fire with insurgents inside of the tree line 50 meters southeast of them.

PEDRO 56's copilot later said they were being hit at the worst possible time. A patient was being brought in by their PJs, with members of the 101st Airborne stuck directly in front of their gunner's .50 caliber.

Racing us around to enter our gun pattern, I checked my game plan with the crew mid-turn to set up the pattern in between our wingman and the insurgents, asking them to fire into the field behind the insurgents if unable to see or target anyone. There was no way we could get an angle to hit them so close.

"Word." Dee signed off with her trademark west coast approval.

"Right's set." Brack's weapon was pushed full forward in anticipation.

"Left." Andy was, of course, ready.

I snapped out of our turn onto the gun pattern heading. Brack opened up with his weapon while I slowed back the last 10 knots as gingerly as a motorist braking in front of a policeman. I wanted to be as steady as possible so he could target more accurately. The enemy fire kept up its intensity, but at least some of it was now being drawn away by us.

I counted down the last seconds of this pattern, then called, "Out."

Banking left, I dove us down to gain airspeed and energy for the re-attack. I wanted to use the short desert trees for any concealment possible with our tail so exposed.

Rolling right and pulling us up to 150 feet while slowing back, our helicopter shook non-stop in a loud rattle, threatening to fall out of the sky, but it still gave more. I absolutely loved this aircraft.

Vulnerable, exposed, and slow we hit our target airspeed of 80 knots close enough to 150 feet as I snapped out our last degrees of bank. Andy's .50 caliber took almost all of my cross-check away as he opened up with our return fire.

The sonic boom of the muzzle was so violent and powerful when full forward that it messed with every pitot static instrument, the non-digital gauges that operate from air pressure. Muscle memory and a seat-of-the-pants feel were in charge without airspeed or altitude instruments mid-gun pattern.

Forever and a day I kept us uncomfortably hung out on this run, trusting in our gunner while our wingman got set with the patient. PEDRO 56, finally ready and needing no approval, hauled every ounce of power, ripping out of the LZ as I dove down one last time to put our guns between them and the threat. With a slight left turn to the north, our wingman closed the gap between us.

Flying across the Green Zone, through the desert, swinging back and forth on our BDAs, all of it was a blur. I don't remember landing at Khandahar Airfield afterwards, either. My first definitive memory was when we were finally on the ground.

"We got holes." Brack surmised, prompting our shutdown.

Somehow, this was our last mission of the day. Our replacements showed up just after that and put their gear on our lone spare aircraft.

* * *

Looking back, I can't explain how helpless these missions felt. Orbiting overhead, unable to see or hit anything yet firing anyway. This was likely the moment when I took on negativity as a best friend. I felt a deep, sinking emptiness, and it simply never left.

Slowly, that emotion took over all background noise, adding a dark shade to my every perspective.

# CHAPTER 4

# ANXIETY, ANGER, DEPRESSION...
## *(...Lather, Rinse, Repeat...)*

### LAS VEGAS, NEVADA, FALL 2010

Welcome home. So much noise. So many unknowns. In between the clamor was awkward, loud silence filled with unasked questions.

Nothing was where I left it, nothing was how I wished it to be. I was not who, or what, anyone else wanted me to be. For me, the changes were overwhelming, for my wife and two kids, expectations went unmet, and there were more questions than answers.

After so long, so many satellite phone calls with children that ended to the sound of a brick's squelch, that single word, *Scramble*, and then a click, who *wouldn't* have questions? Day after day, with all of the behavior changes, who wouldn't *need* to know about what was going on from a family member? From my perspective, though, I had no answers to anything. My memories had only recorded, and I was incapable yet of translating anything to speech.

I'd spent most of the past year on deployment, considering myself a taxi or ambulance driver at best. I refused to even glance in the direction of my experiences or emotions during this entire time. All hardships were dismissed with humor that had begun as a deep gray and only gotten darker with time. Asking me anything about what I was protecting (but refusing to admit I was protecting) resulted in uncontrollable outbursts.

The commotion of kids being kids sent me through the roof. The running upstairs that others enjoyed as the cute pitter-patter of little feet registered for me as an immediate threat and resulted in a jump or a loud curse. Even sitting at the dinner table was too much. I did it for one night and could only stare into space.

I'd seen a bit of my kids in every child we rescued. Now, I was unable to not see their faces in my children. More than once I actually thought I...well, there simply is no proper way to describe having smelled a young burn victim when going to kiss my children.

While deployed, I'd spent a lot of time focused on how great life would be when I got home. The nostalgic, romantic notions of 1950s America sums up how my imagination played it out. Every day my thoughts tried to ignore the combat around me and instead envision how good it would be there.

*Here.* I corrected myself constantly.

I figured this would be how the Pope would feel if it turned out heaven was fake. Prayers for me were useless, and unknowingly I had changed. I had no idea how to be happy without being happy in-spite-of-something.

The expectations of others revealed themselves to be incorrect assumptions, as increasingly they left each person in the household unfulfilled. For me, the air hung heavier by the day as the questions transitioned from the past now behind me to the present inside of me.

*Why are you so quiet? Why do you just stare at your kids? Why do you only sleep for two or three hours?* The handful of times any of these questions were asked was in no way offensive. Yet the body language that accompanied every second in between soon became unbearable.

Somehow, the slow build-up eventually became too much. My mind began translating any question, asked or unasked, into an attempt to control me. I soon lost all patience with any authority, imagined or real. The sad part was I had no idea why.

* * *

"I can't believe the mountains. They look..." My voice trailed off as I gazed in wonder driving home from dinner. *...they look like the mountains north of Khandahar Airfield.* My internal dialogue finished the thought for me.

My son's biopsy had been the day before, and my family and I had just finished eating dinner out together for the first time in months at a local brewpub.

"Like you've never seen them before?" My soon-to-be ex-wife laughed.

She was obviously amused at my fascination with the dusty mountains, which were the same as they'd been on the day we moved to Las Vegas more than a year prior.

I didn't answer. I stared out the window as she drove us home. In retrospect, I don't think I *could* respond because I didn't know what to make of her humor aimed at something that hit me so personally.

I was beyond pissed off for some reason. But I also felt something else I couldn't quite understand.

My wife and I had met as teenagers, when I was 19 and finishing my freshman year at the Air Force Academy. Dating off and on throughout the rest of my time at the Academy, we married after graduation and moved into an officer's lifestyle together. We were together through flight training and, eventually, seven moves in eight years. Along the way, we had two beautiful children, and despite having been apart for most of the past few years, I held to the belief through it all that I wanted nothing more than to be home with them.

So, no, I didn't understand my feelings at the time. It is bizarre, though, because, looking back, that moment is so clear to me. That was when I made up my mind to leave my family.

* * *

## LAS VEGAS, NEVADA, SPRING, 2011

> *Don't ever send me another picture of them. Don't ever send anything about them to me. Tell them I'm dead...I don't care.*

Slamming my phone down, I mashed the truck into gear and left the depressing, stucco-covered office building. I wish I could say this was the first time I'd texted these ugly things, and I wish I could say it was the last. It was neither, and the truth is, I have no idea how many times I told my children's mother to cut me out of their lives.

My tires screeched on the burning asphalt as I turned onto the main road. Moving only a couple of miles per hour out of the parking lot, I understood why the black rubber cried out in pain: being forced to sit in this kind of heat was pure torture.

That day was my first mental health appointment, and I was sure it did more harm than good. I had no idea where I was going and less of a clue what to do after I arrived there. I wasn't sure when I'd gotten to this exact point, but the last few months had been more than I could bear.

Not too long ago everything made sense. Living in Afghanistan, things were simple. Run when told; fly like I knew how; drink lots of water, even if it was poison; and do anything it takes to have fun with my best friends.

The day I found out my son was sick was a Saturday and I was in Afghanistan. By Monday morning, I was stateside, in the middle of my son's bone marrow biopsy.

One of my last clear memories of that time was my kid screaming in harmony to the drill. The medical staff shouted unintelligibly as I ran out of the operating room into the blinding sunlight of Las Vegas. I don't think I've been sober or happy for more than a few hours at a time since then.

On a positive note, it turned out when the doctors thought my son had cancer, well, those were apparently just opinions. Shortly after the bone marrow testing, the results came back negative for leukemia. However, that good news didn't fix any of his issues.

After the sixth straight month of battling mysterious fevers, when my child's temperature soared above 105 degrees every single day, he was at some point diagnosed with Periodic Fever Disorder. The prescription was simple: *Keep a watchful eye on him.*

For those lacking experience with medical professionals, this was the official way of saying, *We have no idea what's wrong with him, but good luck.*

Within another six weeks of me being home, the fevers went away almost as suddenly as they'd appeared. That nice turn of events, combined with my leaving on a months-long training trip, allowed me to not deal with any of it. I had no idea what the main point of anything related to that military classroom course was, but it was a welcome reprieve from my home life.

Everything for some reason made me so upset. I'd been home for less than two months before the training trip, but I could hardly look at my kids without crying during that time. I kept seeing the patients we picked up.

My entire life had become one big emotional reaction. Anxiety told me there was a threat the second I woke up in the morning. With no awareness of my behavior, I turned my mind into a built-in subconscious big brother. It felt only one thing: a need to protect itself nearly every waking moment.

In other words, my anxiety translated to always searching for anything that *could* be wrong. And I became enraged whenever I found that something.

*That's what's wrong, that's what's going on.* This became my mind's hidden mantra as it sought to protect me from some unknown evil.

The reason for my irritation could've been anything, or nothing at all. No matter how small or unknown, a simple pet peeve could set me off for the rest of the day.

Whenever I was finally able to let go of that anger, whether it be hours, days, or weeks later, depression set in, and I switched from unknowingly looking for threats to actively begging for death to make it all end. The worst part was, nobody told me it was happening or that it was going to happen. It just did.

I had begun drinking even more heavily and hanging out in local Vegas bars as a way to get away from it all. I felt safer there, even though the opposite was true. Although a lot of people always milled around, I had no clue I was avoiding others. However, that was the truth. I was isolating myself, even in public.

Part of me began to recognize this, though. In April of 2011, some friends and I stayed late after a unit party at a local casino. The party ended at 1:00 in the morning, but we ended up reminiscing, drinking, and crying in the middle of the casino until daylight for no reason. We just kept talking about dead friends while sobbing in public, all night long.

That night convinced me to call a mental health professional, and here I was. Unfortunately, I wasn't able or willing to accept the help offered. I had no way of understanding what was going on with me.

*Fuck it* doubled as an expression and a pathetic mindset. In reality, it was an empty attempt to not care about the direction my life was headed. But that kind of attitude never puts anything to bed.

I thought about the time I'd just wasted. The poor lady sitting in front of me was some random social worker who had been assigned to me through a free, and more importantly, discreet program outside of base. She had no idea what to think.

"Why would anyone do that to a child?" she'd cried after learning about some of our missions.

Her question meant she refused to accept such evil existed, but it royally pissed me off. A car horn jolted me out of my daze as I realized it was my turn to go.

*She didn't even give me any instructions, didn't tell me anything to do.* I merged onto the highway and found yet another problem with her.

I didn't even know where I was driving to. But I knew I didn't want to sit at home. I'd been doing that ever since last month's party.

The silence of the truck cab brought me back to the present as I complained aloud to myself, "Nothing to do..."

However, that was obviously a lie, as the appeal of the environment evidenced. A local bar with video gambling called my name from a distance, and I increased my speed a few miles an hour above the speed limit to prove it. In reality, I was out to do anything to take my mind off the painful therapy session I'd just left.

*Why would anyone do that to a child...* My mind repeated the question as a statement.

A sinister laugh and a shake of my head was a weak attempt at dismissal. *There was no point to any of it. It was all pure evil.*

Billboards flew by, competing with one another for attention. *Look at the overcrowded advertising space we used to call air.* I tried making myself laugh, but somehow, even that and the flashing fluorescents were not enough to keep me distracted. *Why would anyone do that to a child...*

*Don't go there!* I turned on the radio to some hard rock station and hit the gas, weaving in and out of traffic. I couldn't even remember what had originally inspired me to talk with this lady about it in the first place.

*Yes, you do.* Red-hot guilt flooded my body as pictures of my kids entered my mind, pictures texted to me right before the appointment.

*I told her not to send me any more pictures. It's not my fault!* My mind's defense against itself was successful as I attempted to let go of the mental dialogue for a minute.

Soon, however, the anxiety crept back in. I wondered what the counselor thought of our conversation.

*She didn't care at all.* I twisted the memory of a glance at the clock into a lack of concern.

On board the emotional train, this ride home started with depression, became guilt, had churned into anxiety, and then morphed into hostility, seemingly in rhythm to the music. *Why did I waste my time? I feel worse than I did before!*

*Because there's not one good thing about that fucking place! Afghanistan is a worthless deathtrap!* Car horns blared at me as I swerved around much slower cars in the express lane with no thought for the safety of others, or myself.

Ruminating thoughts like these seldom had a purpose except to feed the dark side of my psyche, turning the negativity into more of an addiction than any drink or drug.

*Why would anyone do that to a child?...* I had asked that same question before.

I wished I hadn't.

For months now my life had become a cycle of anxiety, anger, and depression. I fell asleep at night by drinking until I blacked out. I left my wife and kids and couldn't even bear to see pictures of my children without crying, let alone look at them when they were standing in front of me.

*They look just like my kids...* The exact thought about our young patients I'd had months before in Afghanistan re-surfaced in a dark memory.

"Why would anyone do that to a child?..." I repeated out loud. *Why...*

\* \* \*

> *At first, I did not understand any use of or discussion involving myself and the term PTSD. I assumed that I could not have the disorder because my biggest issues came with memories of the patients, specifically the children, that we were tasked with picking up. I did not care too much either way about the combat, although I loved the flying. But, as any psychologist will explain, trauma is trauma.*
>
> *The instant that I began personalizing anything to do with our patients, I unknowingly set myself down the wrong path. Yet again, the trail can be traced specifically back to a handful of missions from Afghanistan in 2010.*

## KHANDAHAR AFGHANISTAN, SUMMER 2010

"Why would anyone boil an infant!" I demanded over the helicopter's intercom.

I didn't want to hear an answer to that question, but I couldn't stop myself from asking another, "How do we even know it was on purpose?"

That day was our first mission picking up a child that had been intentionally boiled alive, per the Nine Line (the name of the medical mission requirement/authority). Supposedly, insurgents had begun finding new inspiration in their methods to frighten locals from helping ISAF. I was about to be indoctrinated further into the reality of warfare.

"Oh, now you want my expertise, huh?" Our PJ Team Lead sarcastically threw out.

He was still a little upset with me for not letting him cut my hair during the last dust storm and was enjoying letting me know it. He thought I didn't trust him, but in reality, I just wanted to see what the Russian women in the Khandahar barbershop were like. (Turned out they all looked like my old Georgia grade-school bus drivers from the 1980s. Slightly different accents, though...)

"It's the pattern of burns, mano." He was no longer laughing. "If it's an accident, flames and liquids are a lot more random, burning the victim disproportionately. When it's not an accident, the kid pulls his legs up, protecting the bend of the joints, like the back of the knees.

"The same thing happens up the front side of his torso, destroying the more delicate skin of the groin and genitals and stops near the nipples, below where the fucker was holding him under the pits. I guess they don't care about melting a baby's skin off, but those pussies don't want to hurt their precious fingers."

The PaveHawk helicopter had a weird way of making things sound different than normal. Any quiet laughter, agreements, or comments were never keyed up to the intercom because, well, it sounds stupid pressing the mic to hear yourself giggle or mutter. It also made conversations like this sound beyond twisted.

"Hey, Rob, check out Masam Gar real quick." Dee changed the subject to the FOB we were flying toward.

Or so I thought. She held up a crumpled drawing that was more akin to a child's version of a pet robot than anything resembling a flight pattern.

"What the hell am I looking at?" I cracked up trying to make sense of what she showed me.

"God! You are the worst draw-er ever!" Andy turned toward the picture.

He went back to manning his weapon, hanging halfway outside the helicopter. We were gliding the side of a ridgeline at 120 knots.

"Did you just call her a draw-er? I think you mean artist, numbnuts!" Brack was never one to miss an opening to tear down his gunner.

Sitting back with the rocks and sand zooming by outside his window, he came off more like a high school bully throwing wadded up homework at a friend than a combat aircrew member slinging his .50 caliber cannon around in the wind stream.

I had us riding what is known as a military crest. That is, flying a third of the way down and as tight as possible to a mountain ridge. The ridgeline that we were currently surfing ran southwest from Khandahar City toward our mission objective, a mutilated baby. I dove our aircraft further down the mountain to keep us tucked in, which kept my eyes focused outside and unable to study the image closely.

Dee, trying hard not to laugh, continued pointing. "Yeah, I've been here before. You want to swing around...and then..."

Her voice described our path yet still trailed off as I lost focus.

"I'm not gonna lie, Dee. I have no idea what the hell you just said." I admitted without a hint of shame.

I was exhausted from the pace we'd been maintaining. The oppressive heat and the patients were starting to take it out of me. I'd learned that being angry or making jokes made it feel like things weren't bothering me, in the short term, anyway.

What was worse, I obviously didn't care about what was going on around me. I wasn't sure anymore why we were here, but I was certain our overall mission was bullshit. Winning hearts and minds was about the stupidest wartime objective I'd ever heard. And I was damn sure tortured kids weren't supposed to be part of this fucking deal.

"Here, look at this for a minute, and I'll fly." She recognized my attitude was sinking.

Anxiety, Anger, Depression...

Laughing and picking up the copy of a caveman etching I was somehow supposed to glean information from, I attempted to recognize the flight pattern she was talking about.

After a minute, I simplified things and decided, *Fuck it, I'll figure it out when we get there...*

"Got it. Thanks." I stuffed the note into a random pocket and took back the controls, while my mind drifted again to the patient.

Dunking male infants into boiling water hits tribal lifestyle pretty hard. Disabled males, especially boys who can't become fathers, instantly lowered the family's social standing. If he's the only child, it becomes the death of a bloodline.

Glancing inward at the GPS, the range to Masam Gar was closing to three miles, so I readied myself for the approach.

The entire crew was more quiet than usual for this one when Dee spoke up. "Dude, you wanna slow it down a bit."

I took her guidance and pulled it back to 100 knots but didn't want to give in any further. *This is way too far out to begin the approach.*

I reasoned she probably didn't remember what was on the other side of this ridgeline and kept more power applied than what she'd hinted at. The Green Zone is labeled so because of the bright green growth along either side of the river, which contrasts with the barren desert surrounding it. In both Afghanistan and Iraq, the river areas are teeming with life and are usually labeled Green Zones.

There's even a U.S. base in Baghdad, Iraq, called *Green Zone* — the one that famous movie was named after. For that matter, soldiers have probably always named riverbeds some version of that name since the beginning of time.

This was one of the few exceptions, however. The other side of this mountain ridge was the Black Zone, so named because insurgents were in control there. You didn't overfly if you didn't have to. Last week we had no choice but to cross and had taken fire as penance. I had no desire to repeat that.

We were about to lose our ridgeline of protection, and I was planning on keeping our airspeed up to make it in quicker. Tensing, I waited for the terrain to drop off our right side so I could take power out and roll into a descent with it, finishing low and fast into the LZ.

The problem was, I hadn't listened when Dee tried to tell me how to get in, because there was only one way in. We were about to come within sight too high, with not enough room to make it straight in.

*Fuck!* I screamed inside as I realized this too late. Masam Gar was way too low, and we were coming in way too fast.

What was worse, it was wedged in between the end of our ridge and another one running the same direction. Not only was there one way in, there wasn't any room to dump this energy we had and descend. Changing gears and circling to lose altitude was now the fastest option.

"That's what I was trying to tell you." Dee was pissed at hanging out up there longer than we had to.

I said nothing and hurried the rest of this landing up. It was clear I'd put us all at risk, and the threat was too real to bother discussing it anymore. Not now, anyway. I'd never felt more hatred toward myself than at that moment. The feeling tore at me as I rolled out from our turn and pulled more power in on short final for the approach.

Transitioning above the packed sand and dirt to the gravel in the LZ, a light brown-out consumed us before touching down, dust taking the shape of our rotor then dissipating almost as quickly as it had appeared.

I called over the inter-plane frequency, "PEDRO 55 is wheels down."

"PEDRO 56 copies, holding south." Our wingman broke left out of the gun pattern and headed for the desert calm.

Within a second of touching down, our team was out the door. Watching the PJs rush to the small group of soldiers surrounding a medic, the father, and the baby, I felt even angrier at myself for screwing up. It had added only seconds, but still, that damn *What if?* ate at me.

Soon, the team was heading back with the patient, and it was time to drop any concern for what had gone wrong. Break was over, it was time to get to work again.

"PEDRO 55, 30 seconds to takeoff," I called our wingman to cover our takeoff.

"PEDRO 56," our Chalk 2 aircraft answered.

Almost immediately after the cabin door slammed shut behind me, I felt sick from the smell. I had to choke back the revolting taste filling my mouth.

Dee first put words to the experience. "Ugh, that's awful!"

*Holy shit...that kid smells like a branded cow!* My thoughts were much more specific as the stench of cooked skin cut through the already overpowering odor of gas, exhaust, and metal.

The clock I should've been referencing for the takeoff brought itself to my attention. *Was that 15 seconds or 25?*

I crept in power to just below takeoff and felt the aircraft get light on the tires.

*Fuck it, that's 30.* I ripped all our remaining power in and crosschecked the rotor, the engines, the heads-down display, the radar altimeter, and the outside as quickly as possible in a constant pattern until we were safely away from the ground.

Shortly after takeoff, I found myself suppressing any thoughts of that smell and where it was coming from. I couldn't believe how similar this kid was to my own. His face was colored a light olive, almost pale underneath. Soft, brownish-black hair fell back to reveal a pale, young face…too young for these experiences.

Twenty-five minutes of breathing it in later, we were wheels down at the hospital pad, dropping off the father and patient. For as much as I looked forward to getting away from them and taking the short flight to the re-fuel pits, I'm not sure I ever let this one go. The smell and the taste absolutely consumed me.

Instead of chastising me for what I'd done, Dee tried to brighten the mood. She understood and wanted to help, but it was hard to concentrate on humor with the presence of that lingering stench. I assumed it would go away after re-fueling, but it never did. Knowing why the kid was suffering killed any comedic attempts, so we sat in silence.

It was all so…I don't know, maybe Dee said it best. It was just so…*Awful*…in every way.

As Andy and Brack disconnected the fuel and static (electricity grounding) lines, I thought more about that reason why. *What are we doing here? Why was this child tortured?*

I should've been paying more attention to the aircraft weight and the wind. My mind was taking it easy this mission, apparently, but the laws of physics were not.

We'd added nearly 2,000 pounds of fuel, and the temperature outside was now more than 120 degrees. These things combined meant we had power to land into the wind, and into the wind only. Unfortunately, the wind was dying down to a light breeze, making it harder to discern the direction we needed to takeoff and land into.

"FE is up," Brack announced after jumping back onto the bird and plugging in his helmet.

"Gunner's up." Andy chimed in.

"Roger," I replied before calling tower and taking off.

The plan was to land straight to the taxiway, park this beast, and find some cool water. On takeoff, however, my mind trailed off once more to what I was seeing here. For almost two months, we'd been picking up soldiers, men, women, and children...too many children.

*The wind is at our back.* I noticed this between thoughts of our younger patients.

I changed my mind and went with a 180-degree turning approach. Taking a little power out, I slowed down as we crossed the main runway at Khandahar. Being so mentally exhausted, I was more aware of the shortcomings of our multi-nation coalition than I was that the wind was, in fact, mainly coming from the original direction: I was trying to land with a tailwind.

All four members of our crew were suffering from this pace, this mission. Amazingly, not one of us paid any attention or noticed a thing, until...

*WHOOP! WHOOP! WHOOP! WHOOP!*

The rotor's low speed horn wailed, warning me that we were losing power rapidly.

Pausing reality, we were 100 feet in the air, turning right at 30 degrees of bank with not enough speed to do so without falling. We also didn't have adequate engine power to stop the turn and the fall at the same time. We were about to drop, well, as fast as 20,000 pounds can plummet from 100 feet.

You see, helicopters always maintain a constant engine speed. The flight controls actually change the pitch, or angle, of the rotor blades (to push more/less air down) while the engines speed up or slow down, similar to a car's cruise control. I simply didn't have the power for how much pitch was needed.

Anyone who's ever had a car engine's RPM run into the red and tried to accelerate beyond its maximum can attest to what happens next: revolutions per minute decrease in helicopter engines similarly to cars. Remember our speedboat-on-the-water example? Per the laws of aerodynamics, I'd just taken the boat onto the edge of Niagara Falls.

*Fuck, get it level!* I berated myself, fighting the aircraft over the noise of the horn.

I threw the cyclic to the center, slammed the collective down to take out power, and fixed my eyes on the only thing that mattered, rotor speed. I had the rest of my life, or approximately four seconds, to fix this colossal fuck-up.

Falling out of 100 feet sideways, we had no power and seemingly no chance to recover this crash. Through 50 feet we fell, 40, then 20. Ground rush came up faster than I had ever experienced.

After stabilizing rotor speed and centering the stick, I yanked the collective as high as possible without losing rotor speed a second time. I cared about two things: keeping rotor speed and getting the aircraft level for this last countdown. My eyes flew back and forth. Rotor, level, rotor, level, rotor, level...

*SMACK!*

The wheels hit at nearly the same time, the shocks absorbed much more force than usual, but they miraculously didn't fail. Somehow, I'd landed us flat and stopped enough of the fall with cushioning from the rotor.

"Holy— Is anyone hurt?" I could barely verbalize the question.

"What the fuck was that!" The crew seemed to question all at once.

"PEDRO 55, do you need crash/fire assistance?" The Khandahar Tower controller had even noticed.

*Holy shit...even Tower saw that!...They must've thought we lost an engine or something.* This idea turned me solid crimson.

"PEDRO 55, negative, we'll take it up with Ground Control," I called back, every word hurtful to say.

"Guys...I...I'm so...I don't—" I could not even begin to apologize to my crew. "Dee, your flight controls..."

I couldn't taxi in. Sure, nothing had happened, in the end. *But we almost...*

I had no explanation, no clue how to think about this one mission. *Both landings, both of them. You screwed them up worse than anything in your entire career! Over a thousand flying hours. What the...*

I couldn't comprehend how I'd misread the winds, how I'd lost focus, how any of it could've happened. We taxied in without a word. I sat still, hanging my head. I didn't look up, didn't pay attention to anything. When we stopped, I couldn't even let the rotors quit turning before I ripped off my harness straps, the communication cord, and the rest of my gear. I supposed I should count it a small victory that I wasn't puking all over myself. I'd almost killed my crew, the people I cared about more than anyone else in the world, maybe the only people I truly cared about at all anymore.

*Why? Because of what? Hearts and Minds?* I hated myself for it and didn't say a word as I walked alone to the alert shack.

*Fuck this place. Fuck these kids. Fuck this fucking life...*

* * *

Not all missions were rough. There were even some flights where we were all able to head out to the helicopter discussing most of the known facts ahead of time. One time we made it to the chow hall and scored some awesome breakfast burritos (eggs and ketchup in a stale wrap) before stepping to the aircraft.

To this day, I always hear our Team Lead's voice any time the song *Alejandro* is played. Dee got him singing it somehow, and that dude sang it for a week straight on every flight. I can't lie, though, we all joined in.

Unfortunately, sorties like that were the exception rather than the rule. Instead, the rule was, run first, find out more when you get there.

On the other end of the pendulum were the missions where you had no choice but to land and/or take off under fire, sometimes into an active minefield, and still others into an active minefield under fire. Thankfully, those were also the exception. But when the choice was to either let the injured die or take the risk, was there really a choice to be made?

The worst thing about those missions was even though they didn't happen as often, they usually came in multiples. On bad days we found ourselves going back time after time to the same spots, with few options for different ways in or out.

The funny part was there was no standard mission type. The sorties were more like the proverbial box of chocolates than anything else. Sometimes we got simple patient transfers from one secured LZ to another. A handful of others amounted to simple hospital blood transfers or mental health transports.

On one mission we found ourselves fighting our way in and out of the Black Zone for an Army amputee. Immediately after we'd taken off and gotten away from the area, we were re-tasked a mile further up the river to pick up an ANA (Afghan National Army) soldier who had a sucking chest wound.

After we made it out again, our wingman sent word that this ANA soldier was fine. I even have camera footage of the quarter-sized bruise left from where the round hit his body armor. No, we weren't too happy about sticking our necks out for that clown.

Some of the most bizarre and hilarious events occurred randomly. Brack's favorite was from an earlier mission when his crew picked up a female Marine with excessive menstrual bleeding. Ten minutes later a second patient was added from the same location, a male Marine with blood in his stomach. (In his southern humor, 1 + 1 = hilarious! And he was right. *That's pretty damn funny, right there...*)

Andy's favorite was a mission when he claimed to see a local having relations with a goat (sorry, brother, I'm still not buying it). I have to admit I don't have a favorite, though. We had random sorties to pick up the dude who'd gone postal because his wife was cheating on him, and I can't forget the Army bubba who shot himself in the hand with a nail gun. But, no, there really were no number ones for me.

Unfortunately, too many times we'd find ourselves sprinting an eighth-of-a-mile to the helicopter, throwing the blistering gear on, and finishing the start-up only to hear, "Seven-year-old boy, gas burns to 70 percent of his body...arms, torso, legs..."

Those missions tended to rip my heart out. There were no funny parts to them and no good memories from them. Sometimes, we had to fight our way in and fight our way out. Sometimes, our buddies died. I made my own peace with dying and was reminded all too often of the likelihood. We all accepted these outcomes.

But how do you accept a seven-year-old child being doused in gasoline and lit on fire? That's not supposed to happen...

\* \* \*

## CAMP BASTION, AFGHANISTAN, SUMMER 2010

"PEDRO 23, MIST as follows: POI...two local nationals, motorcycle accident; five-pound infant girl severe head trauma, exposed brain matter; 10-pound infant boy severe body trauma, road-rash..." Our controller at MOM said, feeding us new patient info.

The LZ was an unknown once again, somewhere on the north edge of Highway One, five miles past MOB Price, a location nestled in between two of the most dangerous places along the Helmand River.

"Uh, MOM, can we get a radio frequency for these dudes?" Dee's call hid her feelings about the situation.

I, for one, was pissed about not having any communications with the convoy on Highway One that had sent in the mission.

"Negative, PEDRO, contact MOB Price." The dry directive came back.

"Does anyone want to tell those fucktards that MOB Price has a Welsh controller relaying something from a French convoy?" Brack was furious.

"No, he won't know anything about that or be able to help us," Dee replied, reading between the lines that we were stuck figuring this out on our own.

At present, I was on the controls and had us set up a few miles south of the stopped convoy, circling high overhead. We were stuck trying to figure out what some French convoy had told a Welsh guy who was speaking a language known on paper as English.

Right about now would be a horrible time for anyone in the chain of command to make things worse for us, so we held our collective breath when the operator at MOM made a change in plans. "PEDRO 23, the patients need to be taken to Lashkar Gah."

Fury instantly overtook me. "What? What did he just say?"

It was now my turn to burst in on the intercom, demanding an answer that didn't exist. "Why would we take them to Lash?"

The local Afghani hospital, Lashkar Gah, was located in the middle of its namesake town, Lashkar Gah, or Lash, for short (I have no idea if it had a separate name from the town, to be honest). Lash was a minimally staffed, locally-run surgical-ish clinic. But that wasn't what upset me. What enraged me was the fact that Lash had no neurological or pediatric units.

"Dude, we're out of beds at Bastion's hospital," our Combat Rescue Officer informed me from the back.

"So, put them on the fucking floor. They're dead if we take them to Lash!" I cried.

"I know, bro," he stated, kicking his feet in the wind, either not caring about or enjoying my aggressive flying.

Dee felt the same and called back, trying to rectify the situation. I can't remember the exact response on the other end, but we were essentially told to take the two babies to the locals and then to go fuck ourselves.

Come to think of it, Andy probably added the last part.

But Dee had argued until we couldn't afford to waste any more time. We needed to get things moving before the situation got any worse.

"All right, someone in the convoy popped red smoke. We cool with just pressing in?" I noticed the color from the scene of congestion below.

Highway One was backed up for miles in both east and west directions from the wreckage, and hundreds of locals were gathered in a big mass right next to where someone, supposedly a French convoy, had thrown out a smoke grenade marking where they wanted us to land...or shoot us.

We had no idea who threw the smoke or what their situation and intent were. Our standard operating procedure was that red smoke meant the LZ was compromised, don't land.

"We might as well get this shit-show over with," Brack judged. "But I don't think they have a clue what the fuck they're doing."

"I don't think you have a clue what the fuck you're doing." Andy cut in at his Flight Engineer.

Brack couldn't answer, he was laughing so hard from that one. Stealing a glance at the back, I tried to not lapse into hysterics with them. Deep down, though, I knew they felt the same way I did.

"Yeah, whatever, it's hot out, let's get it done." Dee confirmed the plan and briefed our wingman's crew over the inter-plane frequency about what she wanted them to do.

I was still angry about the situation and took this dive excessively steep behind the terrain south of the LZ. In another minute we were circling to land to the southeast, our left tire a few feet from the smoke canister.

The PJ team ran out from under the rotor disc and split up, the CRO getting specifics from the convoy commander while the PJs went straight for the patients. Our Team Lead directed his battle buddy as they took over care for both patients and simultaneously covered each other, well, as much as two guys could cover each other in front of hundreds of locals crowding them. More and more cars backed up in both directions as the traffic kept coming.

The blacktop of Highway One seemed so bizarre, like a river of asphalt cutting through the desert. Waves of heat radiated up like they did back home, but, for some reason, these waves seemed different than the ones in the US.

*Maybe it's the dust.* I shrugged and returned to the rhythm of my never-ending anxiety game... *Where's the threat? Who's going to kill us?*

We all knew where we were and how to get home, or rather, to Lashkar Gah, so no need to run any navigation prep. We had plenty of power and space on the helicopter for the kids. There was nothing to do except sit, waiting for our next cue to jump into action.

I wished for something else, though, wished for something that needed to get done. Mostly I wished I wasn't staring at my friends covering a newborn's brain.

I glanced at Dee, sitting quietly, doing the same thing I was, and I figured she might be feeling the same, too.

A second later she turned to me. "Want me to put Lash in the system?"

I shrugged. "Sure, thanks."

I was grateful to watch her fingers punch in the new coordinates even though there was no need for it. My mind was clearly more relieved to pay attention to others solving useless problems than helplessly witnessing the situation develop.

Picking my head up, I waved the team back in to load the injured children. Notifying PEDRO 24 of our impending takeoff and securing the aircraft took all of 30 seconds before I lightly raised the collective. I increased power for takeoff and got us out of there as gently as possible for the kids.

Head injuries require as little altitude change as possible (due to damaged sinuses and the possibility for further injury). Our

PJs were trying to perform pediatric surgical work in full battle kit on hands and knees using hard black armor flooring in place of a sterile operating table. They needed all the help they could get with steadying their makeshift surgical room.

Ten minutes into the trip, things calmed down enough in the back of the helicopter for the crew to be filled in on the full story. Supposedly, a father had been riding down the highway on his motorcycle with his entire family. His wife, his teenage son, and his infant son and daughter were all on the one bike with him. We didn't know what led to the accident, but he hit the back of a truck, killing the wife. The last anyone saw of him he was running away with the teenage son, leaving the two infants to die on the road.

*Jesus.* Once again, nobody keyed the mic after listening, and the intercom cutting out became a haunting finale to the memory.

In fifteen minutes, we were skimming the rooftops of downtown Lashkar Gah. I'd never heard any reports of dudes taking fire here, but man, it felt like it could happen on any day we flew in.

*Why are there never any people in the street?* I wondered as shacks on top of shacks leaning next to each other zipped by, looking more like a series of apartments made out of cards.

Transitioning to a more realistic place for my mind, I started this approach farther out, which kept the flight smooth going in. I finished with a final slide above the tops of the rusty, aluminum-sided alleyway and over the concrete wall surrounding the hospital's LZ.

Still taking care to treat the aircraft as gingerly as possible, I set us down and finished lowering the collective, taking all power out.

*Ouch!* I didn't realize I'd been gripping the stick and the collective so hard, or that I was soaked in sweat. Peeling my fingers off one by one should've been easier, considering how wet my hands were. I don't think I cared, though, as my mind was set to record. Contemplation was not an option.

I, like the rest of my crew, watched as these newly-orphaned children were taken inside. *Why is it taking so long?*

Maybe I just wasn't used to staring at every last step. Finally, the team, our patients, and a couple of nurses that ran out to assist, made it to the door. We were about to be freed from this torture.

"They're fuckin' dead," Andy stated with finality.

We all agreed, or at least nobody seemed to have a rebuttal. I knew it in my gut, though.

*Why are we doing this? Why are we here?* I wanted nothing more than to yell at our team to go back, grab the kids, and take them to Bastion.

Instead, I offered only silence. I said nothing at all, simply confirmed that the PJs were clipped in before taking off. As harsh as I'd been careful a minute before, I ripped power in and got us the hell away from that cinderblock-surrounded deathbed of a clinic as quickly as possible.

Across the miles-wide Helmand Green Zone, re-fueled, and back at our parking pads within 30 minutes, nobody had anything to say. Sitting in silence, I guess we all had to make up our own minds what to think, or not.

* * *

One of the things that haunts me is, I could never find out if we left those children to die. For most of our flights, I'd consciously tried to avoid learning any life lessons or making decisions about the meaning of missions. This one, however, was different.

I sat down on my rack that afternoon following crew swap, and I intentionally developed another level for despising myself. Rolling onto my side, I ignored the sound of diesel engines, jet noise, helicopters, and whatever other random notes of warfare were thrown into my lullabies, and I thought about this mission over and over.

I personalized the results by dwelling on my memories that day. Weighing our actions, measuring consequences and determining their meanings, I formed individual concepts that would shape me for years.

I surmised my soul had been beaten into submission so long before that I couldn't even put together an argument against leaving those kids. The trained monkey operating on my behalf had never been taught to question things like this.

After affirming these beliefs time and again, I habitually learned to hate and distrust anyone in charge of me with a passion. This emotion eventually spread like an umbrella, shaping into never allowing anyone to have control over anything. Simply put, I set my mind against trusting in other people ever again.

The sad part was none of these beliefs were necessarily true. Maybe I was looking for someone to blame. Maybe I wanted to point the finger for all the wrongs I'd witnessed. I must admit to feeling that *someone* needed to be responsible.

But a man's own perspective is all that counts, and after that day, my personal opinion was I hated everyone, including myself.

# CHAPTER 5

# LIVING TO COPE, COPING TO LIVE

## LAS VEGAS, NEVADA, SUMMER 2011

"*H*oly shit, we got a huge explosion, three o'clock, four miles!" *Brack cried out of the black...*

...My nightly trip across the world always began the same. The nightmares were so vivid, it was as if I'd never left Afghanistan. I was thrown in for the first time, every time, and forced to face whatever my subconscious dug up from wherever...

*...I instantly realized what was going on as Brack talked our crew onto a 200-foot IED blast cloud almost precisely where PEDRO 24 had picked up its last patient. We'd just finished our climb to 2,000 feet over the Arghandab River Valley northeast of Khandahar, once again out supporting COP Nolen all day.*

*"Get that fucking medevac back here now!" The ground commander's blood-curdling scream reverberated over our FM radio set.*

*I've heard this tone before, just never on an encrypted frequency. His call for help sounded closer to an animal about to be killed.*

A dozen different things occurred simultaneously while I turned our formation west toward the mushroom cloud rising from the detonation.

"PEDRO'S hook right, 55 has the lead!" I threw us over in a hard right turn.

But PEDRO 56 had other issues with their Cat Alpha patient, "Request to return to base single ship ... Scoggs, this dude is dying on us..."

Our wingman had no choice but to continue toward Khandahar's hospital, opposite our return to the desert abyss. We were now on our own course, and I needed to confirm nothing with the crew as the aircraft descended through 1500 feet on a sharp solo descent.

"Cleared to strip, see ya brother." I banked as much as I could, cracked in a little more power to control the rotor and pointed our nose toward the ground, allowing us to get lower faster.

Twelve hundred feet, one thousand...

"Clear, down and right." Brack gave his acknowledgment.

"Left." Andy was set.

Meanwhile, the PJs prepared for the Green Zone, the unknown LZ, and the pickup. Eight hundred feet, six hundred...

"LONGKNIFE, PEDRO 55 Flight is splitting single ship, PEDRO 55 is inbound, 500 and below, request overhead fire support..." Dee coordinated our gunship cover then switched talking to the ground commander without waiting for an answer from LONGKNIFE. "Break, Break, PEDRO 55 inbound two mikes out, request patient MIST."

I loved that she was coordinating this in as close to a free fall as I could get us. I loved even more that we held the same mindset on getting low as fast as possible.

Our crew and team were already set, having just egressed the LZ area on the previous pickup by PEDRO 56. We also had to use the same approach and takeoff paths. It was hotter than hell, figuratively and literally, with the temperature still rising for the day, draining our available power. This placed severe limits on how aggressively we could fly in and out. As a result, being low was the best chance we had of delaying any contact with the enemy.

Passing rapidly through 200 feet, my response was to pull power back in and jam the stick even further forward, holding maximum airspeed.

"Uh, triple amputee, tourniquets..." The ground commander's call on FIRES frequency was broken up by an obviously over-whelming situation.

I rounded out our descent and followed the terrain into the valley while the crew didn't seem phased one bit with the situation. Brack and Andy were set, scanning for threats, our PJs in place.

The helicopter shook at maximum airspeed, 50 feet above the desert as I took a sharp left bank around FOB Terra Nova. Ever crosschecking climbs and descents, I pushed our single PaveHawk, which was now loudly announcing our impending repeat approach.

Taking it all in stride, Dee paused this time until I rolled out from our turn, then responded, "PEDRO'S one mike out. Pop smoke! Pop smoke! Pop smoke!"

The ground commander delayed for a second before replying, "Roger, PEDRO. Be advised that the LZ is one field west of previous LZ..."

All of a sudden, a teenage boy we were about to fly directly over, dumped what appeared to be a bundle of wood, dropped to his knee with an RPG, and aimed it right at us.

He disappeared below the glare shield (the helicopter's dashboard) as I had a dual realization: RPG... We're dead.

He reappeared in the chin bubble (the windows on the helicopter's chin) but only for a moment, as everything happened in a *flash at 50 feet and more than 120 knots. I banked right then rolled out in an effort to change our plane and phase of flight, tensing for the concussion.*

*And...nothing blew up. I had no time or ability to turn around and find out or confirm anything else.*

*Thankfully, Dee remained oblivious to what I'd seen and was aware enough to respond, "Confirm new LZ has been swept for IEDs!"*

*I analyzed the smoke and checked the aircraft into a course correction when suddenly I caught on. These fields were littered with IEDs from the past two days, and the Army platoon hadn't searched this LZ!*

*"Negative..." The quiet radio operator trailed off.*

*I stole a glance at Dee as she shook her head. "Just get it over with..."*

Fuck it! *I obviously agreed to this stupid-ass, undiscussed plan to go raging in, as I threw the collective down and pulled the cyclic back. I wanted to put us into the LZ as fast and as low as possible.*

*"Thirty feet, 100 knots," Dee called our approach parameters.*

*"Clear down and left." Andy followed Dee with his clearance call.*

*The call-outs from the crew members came faster and faster. I kept the speed as high as possible on this approach to a landing, not giving into full commitment until the last possible second.*

Slow down, too fast. *The gut feeling took over as I kicked the tail out hard in response, putting us into a nearly sideways slide and using wind resistance to stop us faster.*

*Andy, despite being unable to fire over our friendly forces, stood exposed, almost completely out of the aircraft, scanning for threats and about to take charge of guiding our approach.*

*"Twenty feet, 30 knots, gunner has the calls." Dee passed all communication to Andy, meaning that only he would talk, guiding me down as we passed through twenty feet.*

*Twenty feet was also the magic number I'd predicted in my head for when we'd blow up if there were any IEDs on this approach.*

*Fifteen feet... The radar altimeter displayed in bright green LED lighting,* Maybe now...

*Guess not. I threw the tail back into alignment, hauled in maximum power, and shuddered to a perfect landing.*

*A huge berm was off our front left at 11 o'clock. The platoon we'd been supporting all day was strung out along a small trail leading up to it, not wanting to move, and struggling hard.*

*"Patient's at the 10 o'clock, team's cleared out." My call the second we touched down sent our three-man PJ team out, which left our crew anxiously waiting and exposed.*

*The PJs got to the first patient, beginning treatment while our Team Lead met with the ground commander and worked out details. A second patient with a shredded left hand, shrapnel coming out of his arm, and a concussion was being helped toward our helicopter behind the first.*

*Staring in shock, I broke the unspoken rule to never look and locked eyes with the first patient, a triple amputee, as he was taken in slow motion past my removed cockpit door. This was all so strange.*

*He shouldn't be like this... My mind searched for explanations that did not exist.*

*There was hardly any blood. One stump, packed with dirt and shrapnel, seemed more like a broken tree branch. His eyes, stark white in contrast to his soot-blackened face, were hollow, devoid of life.*

*A member of the platoon ran up and tossed the patient's missing boot onto the stretcher, foot and ankle still inside. His eyes never moved away from mine while time slowed to a crawl.*

*It felt like he was seeing through me.* What's he trying to say? What is...

*Treatment calls began coming through the intercom as confusion set in. Something was missing. We hadn't yet run any pre-takeoff calculations.*

*"Wait, we're not ready yet. Just wait..." I begged for more time, not ready to fly anywhere, not even knowing where to go.*

*In my refusal to accept any more, I somehow detached from the aircraft and those in it fighting to stay alive. The sensation of going from an active participant to a helpless witness became my only keepsake, yet again.*

\* \* \*

### (STILL) LAS VEGAS, NEVADA, SUMMER 2011

*FUCK!* I was ripped out of my nightmare, surprised to be sitting up, shirtless, in bed, sweat gushing from every pore.

*Where is my crew?* I tried figuring out where I was before I started coming back to the present.

*Man, that one again.* My own personal alarm clock wouldn't let me sleep for more than a few hours at a time. The clamor of the helicopter's radio was so loud that my ears were actually ringing from it. Apparently, time has no audible effects on nightmares.

*And yesterday you thought Afghanistan felt like a lifetime ago.* I chastised myself for having allowed any illusion of separation from that shithole, then surveyed my surroundings in an effort to make sure of where I was.

It was pitch black, but my eyes were adjusted enough to recognize I was at home. Even if I hadn't seen it, the sterile Vegas air conditioning set to personal comfort would've clued me in. The added aroma of two-year-old paint on drywall made the place unmistakable.

I'd bounced around during the past few months, starting with the military education course, and then crashed on some friends' couches after separating from my wife. She'd left for her parents' home with our children, and I'd recently moved back to our house on the outskirts of Vegas. The furniture, the bedding, the dishes, the backyard, all of it was the same, yet completely different.

On my first day there, I'd taken everything off of the walls, emptied every drawer, and cleared each countertop. I removed my past, crammed it into storage bags, then hid it away.

Unable to move on, or rather, not allowing myself to move on because of self-inflicted guilt, I'd begun erasing my problems instead of dealing with them. But erasing can only be a lie, and suppression becomes the denied truth. Unfortunately, I was committing myself to learning this lesson the hard way.

Still dazed from the 4,000-mile mindset swing, I stumbled to the bathroom and shook it off the best way I could, splashing freezing water on my face and switching mental gears.

*Time to hit the gym.* I set my mind before recalling I'd walked home from the bar last night.

That nagging feeling continued for another moment until blossoming into full realization. *I didn't come home alone last night!*

I spun around and crept halfway across the tile, unsure of who I'd see. I was able to make out a shape under the blanket.

"Hey..." I hesitated.

I wanted to speak so the girl, who'd seemingly materialized out of thin air, could hear me. I knew that it wasn't even 4 a.m., but I couldn't remember something else...

*I can't believe it. I forgot her name!* I couldn't help giggling as I checked the watch that was all but sewn onto my arm, *3:30. Too soon to kick her out?*

Deciding against it, I figured, *Whatever. I'll be back before she wakes up. Maybe I'll remember her name by then...*

I smirked and dismissed any leftover worries with a simple thought, *Better yet, maybe she'll steal everything and save me the trouble!*

Tiptoeing to the bedroom dresser, I threw on some gym shorts and a shirt, looked down at the stranger passed out on my estranged wife's pillow, turned without a word, and headed for a morning workout.

\* \* \*

PTSD, or any anxiety disorder for that matter, starts off in a relatively understandable manner. No kidding, post-traumatic stress is a healthy response for any human. The word disorder is added after three to six months, when the person doesn't snap out of it.

But what exactly is *it*? What does *it* mean? For me, PTSD began after being taken away from my crew and waking up in a different world while a doctor drilled into my son. But I didn't just sit in front of a mirror, sweating and re-living memories from the past.

Instead, the disorder usually manifested in social situations, or the lack thereof, after a certain length of time. Socially I became selfish, focusing on my own needs, which became fulfilled in the forms of alcohol and women. If alone and not pursuing one of those vices, riding motorcycles, or working out, I was unable to hold back the eventual calling to deal with the traumatic stress I carried around. This was evidenced by sporadic, non-stop fits of anger or bouts of crying.

PTSD is triggered by external factors, but the real distress is in how a person reacts. Many times, a triggering event may simply set the tone for the day. The accompanying feelings, typically anxiety, that result may send the mind into hypersensitive mode, causing it to be on constant high alert. From there, solving the question of what or who is causing the anxiety becomes the hidden agenda of the subconscious.

Personally, I think the most revealing thing about PTSD is the fact that it shows not only how programmable we all are but how difficult it can be for a person to override their own impulses.

On a similar note, PTSD also exposes how hard it is for a person to give up a substance, activity, or behavior that gives them false fulfillment in place of treating the emotional scars. When there is an around-the-clock opportunity for beer, women, food, or drugs, any person needing healing or fulfillment will face difficulty escaping destructive tendencies. As humans, we're slightly more evolved than animals, although it can seem like much less in certain situations.

What happens next is up to the individual person. Some tend toward the depressive side from the start. Some turn to their faith and hold on the best they can.

Others try to fight through it and find out gambling, alcohol, drugs, porn, sex, food, or a combination of substances and behaviors are enough to keep them afloat. For that group of folks, which includes me, lies usually follow in an effort to keep their old life intact while this new, hidden life is in its infancy.

This sounds ominous, but how honest are any of us really? Do most people dish about all of their hardships when asked how they are, or do they simply provide the expected answer and change the subject? That's how easily it becomes to unknowingly enter an addictive lifestyle with PTSD.

\* \* \*

"Yeah, I'm sorry, but I have to leave," I lied to the pretty girl, "I've got to be up early."

I'm awake early every day, but nobody makes me. Instead, I'll be sweatin' to the oldies, thanks to my nightmares. Full disclosure, I'd be missing sleep altogether if not for the grace of beer.

"I'd love to see you sometime, though." My use of the word *love* was stretching it a bit.

The dim glow of the Vegas bar was intentionally meant to make the video poker machines, all built into the bar top, stand out in contrast to any actual life going on around them. The clicking of games, the noisy baseball commentators, and the ringing of the machines barely covered up the truth. Everyone in there sat on a stool, virtually alone, living through pixels. I didn't judge, though, I was buying the lie too.

I handed the girl a borrowed pen, noticing how much the digital screen stood out as she placed a cocktail napkin on it. She underlined the numbers with a cute little curl, while I mentally repeated her name several times before folding the square cloth into my jeans pocket. I thanked her and walked toward the door, not actually caring if I ever saw her again.

A quick glance, a smile back, and the rumbling of my bike that she would get as I left were all part of the routine that kept me busy. Most guys would call me an idiot for leaving then. Sure, I could've stayed and had a good time. I probably could've tried my luck and seen where we ended our first meeting, but that wasn't my style.

Ironically, a day or two wait, and nothing but the truth from here on out was the best policy. And, soon enough, she'd get the truth. I was a combat pilot going through a divorce and not looking to date. Then she'd jump on the Harley with me for a fun evening, while I'd spend the same time postponing my misery for another night. Besides, I was late meeting someone else for drinks. She wanted to finish yesterday's conversation, since I'd left early.

The sad part is, I had no idea how badly I was hurting.

* * *

## LAS VEGAS, SUMMER 2011

After months of putting off the inevitable, I finally agreed to give my marriage one last try. However, after one week, I moved out again.

*Same shit, different day. This time it's for good!* Or so I thought.

Sometime after midnight turned an August Friday night into a Saturday morning, my memory ended. My plans ended. My understanding of who I was ended. What a strange sensation it was, not being present, having a huge gap in my life, and relying on witness statements and hospital reports to write my narrative...

Just after three in the morning, one driver witnessed a motorcycle roaring through an intersection. The bike appeared to hit something in the road, collapsing the front wheel. A driver in front of the motorcyclist heard the accident and hit her brakes. This was unfortunate for the biker, as the back end of his motorcycle had lifted up, and he couldn't stop or turn. The witness watched in horror as the Harley-Davidson Softail smashed into the back end of the SUV, totaling both.

The collision ripped part of the rider's face off, breaking the skull in two places. It also exponentially increased the rotational force of the bike, which became a full-fledged 720 flip. The bike and rider toppled over and bounced 91 feet down the road before coming to a messy halt halfway down the interstate on-ramp.

Thirty minutes later, flashing lights marked the typical urban night scene, statistically more typical on weekend nights such as this. Fire and police vehicles blocked the highway entrance while the ambulance EMTs lifted their unconscious patient into the emergency vehicle.

Slamming the doors shut and jumping up front, the driver of the ambulance glanced behind as he pulled his seatbelt across. His partner had the patient strapped down and gave a ready signal. Twenty minutes later, they arrived at the downtown Las Vegas hospital, off-loaded this passenger, and readied themselves for the next inevitable victim.

\* \* \*

My memory splashed back in the most painful way. The motorcycle rider tried to move but found he could not. Instinctively he fought with the medical staff, having no idea why he was strapped down. That rider was me!

"What is this?" I clawed at the neck collar.

My anger turned to the man looking at me as I reached for him, then it faded away, into the depths, as I was taken over by darkness.

An unknown amount of time later, pain ripped me out of unconsciousness as some other man yanked on my face. The surgery lights were shocking.

*I just want to go away. Get me out of here.* I still had no idea where I was or what was going on. An instant later the pain thankfully forced me into complete blackness again.

* * *

My first clear memory was a couple of days later. Sitting in a wheelchair by myself at the hospital doors, I didn't know what was going on, but my brain was finally working toward catching up.

*I've been released? My wife for some reason is getting the car? I don't remember agreeing to go back to that house.* I had no knowledge of how, why, or even what had happened. The memories were so confusing and they came in like flashes without understanding.

*My bike is destroyed. I remember now.* I was more upset about the loss of my Harley than my own physical wellbeing. I cried when I was told about the bike being totaled and begged for it not to be. Actually, I was told several times, but I kept forgetting. Everything was that confusing to me.

I cried when I saw the wreckage...again pleading for it not to be so. No kidding, I would've been happier not waking up at all than waking up without my bike.

I was devastated, but somehow, I was still alive. My vision was in bad shape, as a skull fracture had broken the shelf upon which my right eye sat.

"Probably no longer pilot qualified..." A doctor had conveniently combined everything into one quick discussion.

Moving beyond my top priorities of motorcycles and helicopters, I also had a broken nose, just above where the tear started. The skin was ripped apart, and the cut went straight down the lower half of my face. The entire right side of my face had been torn open and was now sewn back together.

Various metal pieces and bits of asphalt remained buried in my skin as much of my abdomen had been shredded by the pavement. I had random stab marks and lots of other mysterious injuries, but somehow, I was breathing and in one piece.

In spite of that last fact, I was miserably depressed, and getting more so by the day. I only left the house for doctor's appointments. I became dizzy just walking around because the eye damage left me seeing double. Grounded indefinitely from flying, I felt as if I'd lost a child in that accident.

To make matters worse, I also lost the lifestyle that was keeping my emotions in check, not to mention the fact that I had no idea what damage had been done to my brain. The loss of control over my emotional reasoning should've terrified me.

The sad part is I didn't even care about that. I downplayed every single symptom and did my best to beat any test, specifically by noticing patterns, in order to qualify for a flight waiver. Unbelievably, if I could get enough doctors' signatures, I could fly again.

To get me through it all, I had an endless supply of pain pills. Day and night, I devoured bottle after bottle of opiates, as the legalized addiction conveniently covered up both my physical and mental anguish.

For more than a month following my accident, I hid inside, both the house and myself. I avoided my children; I avoided life.

If I spoke to anyone, it was usually short, and I left no dispute about when I wanted the conversation to end. It wasn't that I didn't love my kids. It wasn't that I hated everyone or everything around me. I thought I did, but that was just an excuse, an explanation to go with my misery. The sad truth was I couldn't be more than what I had inside of me. And what I had inside of me was becoming darker by the day.

It took a few more weeks of guilt, self-hate, and hiding the pain with legal drugs before I made up my mind that I would drive, ready or not. The day after successfully convincing myself I could get around in a car, I grabbed a few things and moved out. This time it really was for good.

Throughout this entire phase of my life, I couldn't deny or excuse two facts: I was unable to question any of my decisions, and I'd lost all care for the consequences.

\* \* \*

*What began as thought patterns of self-protection against unknown/outside threats continued unopposed within my circle of family and friends. While life was easier if I judged others and blamed them for my internal discord as compared to dealing with my own energy, I had no way of turning off that disharmony aside from impulsive behaviors or addictive substances.*

*The resultant pattern of life, for me, became to cope using alcohol or drugs. I began to realize this and play out life without any concern for myself, for that was actually what was causing this newly adopted lifestyle. I didn't care about what I was doing, assuming it was all fucked, anyway. But when did that change for me? When did I lose consideration for myself?*

## KHANDAHAR AFGHANISTAN, SUMMER 2010

"Um, if you haven't heard, Wiz is dead." I forget who said it, maybe our Khandahar detachment commander.

There was no other way to say it, I guess. The Flight Lead and pilot of PEDRO 66, our sister ship, which went down over Sangin, a town in the Helmand River Valley, had died overnight in a hospital on the East Coast. We all knew already, though. Between satellite phones, e-mails, social media, and MiRC chats (a classified military digital chatroom similar to the old AOL setup), nothing stayed secret anymore. We also knew we had to go to work, so this sentence was the extent of the memorial we could give to Wiz.

The brief continued, "All right, PEDRO 55, you guys are taking over the helicopters when the night crews land. We've got an ongoing operation set up 25 miles northwest of FOB Tarin Kowt."

Tarin Kowt, or FOB TK, was a Forward Operating Base a little under an hour's flight north of Khandahar Airfield. The changeover brief continued into mission prep in our stuffy alert shack.

We had to hurry to resume the night shift's mission looking for a gunner's body somewhere along the Helmand River. An Army HMMWV, commonly called a Humvee or Hummer, had been blown up just outside of Firebase Cobra, some outpost nestled in the mountains north of us. They had hit an IED while returning to base, and the missing soldier had been blown clear of the vehicle into the river.

The ceilings of our rickety building hung a foot above our heads, and air conditioners were lined up every few feet along the wall, but they weren't really effective against this oppressive heat.

"Fuck my life," Andy leaned over and whispered in my ear.

He knew this tasking meant supply, re-supply, and more re-supply until we found the body. Combat rescue had ownership over everybody missing in the Afghani theater, which literally meant every body. Pilots, teams, convoy vehicles, anyone who was missing, captured, or killed belonged to us.

"Yep, fuck your life, Andy." I grinned as I scribbled notes and mentally prepared some of the pain-in-the-ass details pilots were supposed to care about.

I couldn't have cared less about anything other than power, however. Nothing here would kill you faster than running out of power.

I felt his pain though. This deployment had started to turn into a twisted, almost surreal cycle with no end in sight. Not long ago, we'd shown up to the news that one of my buddies I'd flown with in Iraq had been shot picking up a Marine out of Marjah, the southernmost town our unit covered along the Helmand River. Now Wiz had succumbed to his injuries.

A couple of days before we'd grabbed a 10-year-old who'd been shredded by RPG shrapnel to the head and torso. The kid was still alive when we dropped him at the hospital pad, but he was torn up so badly it didn't look like there was much reason for hope.

My messing with Andy wasn't just good fun, it was good habit. I knew I was sick and tired of showing up and hearing about friends being hurt or killed. I wanted to know if the news about Wiz was bothering him. Smitty, Wiz's Flight Engineer, was a good friend and had died instantly, along with their three-man team of PJs and a CRO. We still had no idea about their gunner or co-pilot's fate.

The brief finished, and the back-and-forth with the PJs, the gunners, and the FEs began a split-second later.

Likewise, Andy couldn't let me have the last word. "God, who said that you could flap your fucking gums?"

*Yep, he's good.* I chuckled to myself.

Andy was always so happy when he got the chance to say those things to me, which was usually several times a day. I happened to think it was funny as hell too.

"Damn, you need to get some aggression out, don't you, little buddy?" Brack slapped Andy's shoulder, laughing at his own joke.

He joined us in the only fun we were capable of having, comedy at the expense of each other, as we stepped with Dee toward the sound of spinning rotors, dust, heat, mountains, and the start of our July Fourth holiday weekend.

\* \* \*

The noise of screaming engines broke through our intercom as all of our heads spun to the crew chiefs, the airmen in charge of helicopter maintenance issues, flying with us. We were about halfway through our flight north to FOB Tarin Kowt.

Per our regulations (and common sense), we carried two maintenance crew chiefs with us, for those times when we'd be repeatedly shutting down and starting up at other locations. This covered us for when, not if, the aircraft malfunctioned in between flights (which happened the next day, in fact, when the number two engine starter died, but thankfully we were at Tarin Kowt).

"Which one of you dumbasses doesn't know how to work a mic?" Our Flight Engineer's verbal retribution was nearly as merciless as it was instantaneous.

Brack had no tolerance for any screwing around, and zero thought was ever given to hurt feelings in his cabin. "Put that thing up against your lip so we can hear you!"

"No shit, get it up in there!" Andy joined in from his left seat ruthlessly.

I wasn't any better. "Yeah, get it up in there, nice and deep!"

I finished Andy's joke for him without bothering to turn around. Dee couldn't help but crack up as she so obviously enjoyed our little family traditions that had formed in such a short time but felt years old.

"Yeah, man, I'll let you shoot this gun on the way back, but I'm not re-loading these ammo cans in TK," Brack answered the question our crew chief now shouted over the engines instead of risking another mistake with the intercom.

"Yeah, I gotcha, buddy. You're good, we're only having fun." He eased the chief's upset feelings with a chuckle. "Just don't let yourself sound as fucked up as a football bat, 'cause we got nothing else to do."

Brack laughed at yet another question that was being yelled, still afraid of the potential backlash, "All right, check it out, all you need to do is press it up against your face. If you can't feel it, we can't feel you. Know what I mean?"

Staring out at the bleak, rugged, dirt mountains passing by us, I reflected on how I loved our Flight Engineer. He sure knew how to destroy your hopes and dreams if you pissed him off, but he also really knew how to get everyone working for him. He had earned enough respect during his career that only the smallest compliment or approval was necessary.

"Aw, hell!" I suddenly understood this new perspective about my friend in a new light.

Brack had been pulling the same tactic with me: I had begun to work for him, without even knowing it! Smiling to myself and trying to appreciate the fact that it was still below 120 degrees outside, I decided I didn't care and found my thoughts wandering again.

Homemade personal cemeteries were apparently all the rage. Tribal customs were evident on the ridgelines and the shorter, flat peaks above us in the form of body-shaped piles of rocks, complete with sticks holding little flags as headstones. *Parts of life that* National Geographic *never shows you...such a strange existence...* My judgment was more comfortable and important to me than an open mind, apparently.

Minutes later we entered the landing pattern at Tarin Kowt, looking to drop off our maintenance crew chiefs, fill up on gas, and haul the gear to the team that had been out all night. During the landing and the taxiing, the morning heat hit me. The sun wasn't even fully up yet, and the temperature was well over 100 degrees.

By this point, both water bottles I'd stuffed in random places in the cockpit had become boiling hot. I didn't have a choice and elected to drink one of them, anyway. As it turned out, this was a bad mistake. Instantly, I was gagging and spewing water everywhere.

"Every single bottle tastes like melted damn plastic!" I screamed while dribbling a mouthful of hot poison all over myself, failing to spit it out my open door.

The crew burst out laughing, and I couldn't help but join in (even though I was super pissed off). Every pallet of water we could find had been left out on the hot, black Khandahar tarmac for days. And getting more wasn't an option. The few of us who'd tried to drink a bottle of water had ended up with splitting headaches, but if nobody else cared enough to fix the situation. I guessed I shouldn't, either.

"Looks like us Sweaties will have to steal some for you officers later," Andy chimed in, his sarcasm came complete with a chastising cherry on top.

(Sweaties, or Sweat-Es, was a term our enlisted airmen created some time ago because, *The sweaty enlisted do all of the work.*) I knew he'd planned to do it, anyway, but he really enjoyed pointing out the fact that I was now forcing him to do it. This dude knew how to make me laugh.

Quickly re-focusing on the task at hand, I finished running the re-fueling checklists and went through my chicken-scratched notes to input the new GPS fix, or set of coordinates. In the meantime, the Sweaties jumped out and hooked up the gas lines while our maintenance guys ran out under the spinning rotor disc.

Hastily scribbled descriptions of a hill at which the night crew had landed last in the early morning and a handful of numbers meant almost nothing to me. But I'd learned that, as a pilot, I sometimes had to figure it out along the way because there wasn't exactly a 7-Eleven we could run into for directions. The good news was the insurgents in the area had been eliminated, or so we'd been briefed.

I finished cramming the little knowledge I could into my head and stuffed the paper in a leg pocket. As our maintenance airmen ran off to go have fun with their Army counterparts, we signaled to the PJ Team Lead to hop onboard. He'd been waiting for us and was to be our guide in locating the team so we could offload their gear. Minutes later, we'd cleared ourselves out of the small dirt strip airfield and were back to clowning around as soon as we took off on the half-hour flight northwest.

\* \* \*

"So where [the fuck] are they?" Dee demanded the location for our unit's PJ team, her tone dropping the loudest implied f-bomb.

Dee wasn't one to swear, but I think that was because her words could cut deep enough without cursing. We'd just been waved off of the landing zone that the previous night's crew had been using. Literally waved off, as in, having no communications with the JTAC, so some joker ran out throwing his arms around. Apparently one of the other teams in charge of perimeter security had taken over the LZ.

For some reason, tired, missing, or otherwise, the JTAC manning the radio didn't care to answer us as we called time and again. Circling over the southern hills of the sharply descending river valley, we needed to offload our equipment and get out of the terminal area post haste. This wasn't a good place to hang out.

"Hey, you don't have to worry, Pilot. Tier-One dudes were doing backflips into the river down there..." Our Team Lead somehow thought using military slang for top special operations teams, or name-dropping, would help us out.

Dee and I didn't even need to share looks to understand he had no fucking clue where his team was on this mile-long stretch of river we were borrowing from the insurgents. Nothing pisses pilots off more than listening to empty words from someone trying to make things seem not-so-bad. That day, as we searched for the searchers with their lost leader, carrying a small inflatable boat and scuba-diving equipment in the most land-locked country in the world, we had no stomach for bullshit.

We found ourselves stuck following the Team Lead's simple instructions. "Hey, turn right here. I think that's... No, that's not them..."

Our helicopter trolled up and down the river at 50 feet, searching for anyone who wanted the gear we had. At that point, I no longer cared who that was. Additionally, we still had no love from the JTAC controlling the airspace there, so we had no choice but to continue.

"What a cluster-fuck!" Andy, as usual, summed up our situation the most eloquently.

"VS-17, 4 o'clock for 50 meters, cleared right for your approach!" Brack finally managed to spot our team with the aid of a bright orange, foldable survival signal called a VS-17.

Crouching in a hastily prepared LZ along the north side of the river, apparently the PJ was too nervous about something to even pull the orange panel fully out of his pocket.

"I'm blind to the LZ, let's just get this stuff to them." I offered no resistance to getting in and out immediately, with zero concern as to what the landing looked like.

"Aircraft's clear down and left, gunner's blind, don't fuck this up." Andy's support would've given most pilots a heart attack, but to us, it was good, old-fashioned family fun.

Sharply banking us over and rolling out with complete trust in our FE's guidance, Dee soon had us wheels down, in spite of a massive brownout taking away all visual low and slow at 40 feet. (I'll happily admit, I've flown with a lot of pilots who couldn't have made that landing).

Less than a minute later, all of the gear was unloaded, and the team was waving us out of the LZ. They first hauled the boat to the river, anxious to find the missing soldier's body. We wanted nothing more than to get the largest target in the area out of there. The brownout took everything away again as the call-outs by our back-enders led Dee through the blind take-off.

Suddenly, the JTAC woke up or somehow remembered he owned the FIRES frequency. "PEDRO, you're taking fire. Get out of there!"

The shots fired at us killed our takeoff communication sequence (but thankfully none of us) as we strained to see through the dust cloud, not wanting to interrupt any more notice of whatever was coming at us. We were still enveloped in a solid brown cloud as I fought the repeated urge to look for threats, making sure to keep my attention inside the helicopter. It was a toss-up as to what was more dangerous right then: taking off in a complete brownout or the insurgents targeting the dust cloud that was visible for miles.

"...radio check!" Suddenly an unknown person on our satellite communications frequency interrupted out of nowhere, throwing one more wrench at us.

(This would've been confusing had we not all known the exact source of the interruption. The Department of Defense only paid for one frequency for all of Iraq and Afghanistan, and our peers in Iraq had picked this precise moment to check their radios.)

An argument erupted on SATCOM as Dee's normally calm temper went to the extreme. Our Iraqi-based counterpart had no clue what was going on and refused to obey her *Get (the fuck) off!* directive.

I had no desire to listen to anyone's reasons for anything right then, so instead I gave up to handle the bigger issue first.

"SATCOM's off!" I killed our radio with the utmost anger at the timing of the call.

"Motherfucker..." Andy's near-simultaneous rage was cut short as he searched through the brown veil for the threat.

His response was understandable and expected. *None of us mind radio calls from a thousand miles away while getting shot at in a brownout!* I thought to myself.

The dust cloud finally disappeared to our backs as we surged forward through translational lift (a physics phenomenon where a helicopter begins to outrun its own rotor downwash. This results in much less power being used in forward flight than in a stationary hover). Speeding away, we climbed up toward our heavy friendly presence protecting the south side of the river.

Thirty seconds and another mile further from the threat, we all relaxed about what had just gone down. We'd always heard about this happening to other crews, but this was a first for us. SATCOM radio checks in a brownout while taking fire.

"How about we get out of here and debrief this shit-show back at TK?" Brack polled the crew.

"Yes, let's." Dee agreed, with a blend of sarcasm and anger.

"Way ahead of you." I'd already swapped my radio selector to coordinate off the frequency.

"I'd say that'd be pretty goooood." Andy laid out his thickest possible Mexican-American accent.

This set me laughing in the middle of my transmission, putting the rest of the crew in hysterics. All of us were more than happy to be just the crew again, and the aircraft became much quieter and less tense after we changed frequencies. I glanced at the thermostat, wishing the temperature would stay cooler in the low 100s, yet knowing we still had hours more heating up to go.

*There is nothing out here...complete desolation.* I observed my environment in an attempt to change my internal channel.

Thankfully, most of the mountains were a little lower in this area, otherwise we might've struggled to make it over the terrain at all. The extreme temperatures made it difficult for us to climb very high, take off or land at times. We could easily find ourselves in a tenuous position with these conditions, even down at Tarin Kowt's 4,500-foot elevation, similar to the river valley that we had just left. Flying over the rolling, bumpy mountaintops, I knew we couldn't land if anything happened. We simply didn't have the power.

After a short flight to get gas and standby for search or supply requests, Tarin Kowt's valley opened up before us. We each breathed a sigh of relief at the chance for a break, no matter how short. I was happy to see the crew chiefs sprinting out to greet us, their tan short-sleeved shirts soaked in sweat. They were probably as miserably hot as we were, but I was jealous of them wearing less all the same.

"Good God, those short sleeves look sexy!" Andy joked as we taxied to a stop.

I laughed inwardly at how in-sync our thoughts were but didn't have the energy to make a conversation out of it.

"Not as sexy as some clean water," Brack quipped.

We finished shutting down the engines and dragged ourselves toward wherever the Tactical Operations Center was.

\* \* \*

"Oh, shit!" Dee demonstrated another rare exception to her habit against swearing.

I was face-first into a bag of tuna, scarfing down my favorite MRE (meal-ready-to-eat). The term favorite only meant it had the original packaging. We sat inside the normal darkness of any TOC: plywood walls, clunky metal desks hosting cheap government computers, with information being simulcast on 10 gigantic flat-screen plasma televisions.

*Plywood walls with plasma TVs...in the middle of a war... These rooms look ridiculous.* The absurdity of the situation was my sole outlet for entertainment.

Like every other TOC in theater, each TV played 24/7 Pred-Porn, a facetious expression used to describe the drone video feed service members stare at for hours, days, or entire deployments. The camera was first mounted on a Predator drone, the original widely-used unmanned aircraft, hence the term, Pred-Porn.

That day's Pred-Porn showed a team, our team that we'd just dropped off all of the search gear to, uselessly chasing their zodiac inflatable boat down the river as it was being washed away. I was unable to keep from laughing and hanging my head at the same time.

Dee vocalized what I'd joined her groaning about. "Looks like we have to go get another boat..."

"Fuck my life. This holiday totally sucks," Andy chipped in as we all stood ready, pointing to a flyer on the wall.

The flyer announced we should stop by some random unit later today for grilled steaks in celebration of July Fourth. Apparently the Army unit had gotten hooked up and wanted to share. However, the start time was hours after we'd be gone.

*He's right. What a kick in the teeth.* I smiled at the tease and shuffled toward the heat with my crew.

"Boy, those 10 minutes in the A/C really flew by." I muttered, enjoying the chuckles as the heat hit us all like a punch to the face.

By the time we landed back at Khandahar for crew-swap hours later, all four of us were wiped out. Nobody complained, though, we didn't have the energy.

Listening to my stomach grumble, all I cared about was finding some food. I walked to the maintenance shack, where plastic crates of food-ish stuff, known as Mermites, were delivered daily, and opened one massive side door. Judging by the recent history of unidentifiable food-type things, I shouldn't have been surprised, but somehow, I was.

"Yo, Andy, check out this yard-bird!" I pulled out what appeared to be chicken, had it been the size of a pit bull.

"What is this? It looks like a femur from one of those toddlers we picked up last week!" I exclaimed.

"Holy..." Andy almost dropped his cardboard tray, trying to hold on while shaking from laughter.

I had no idea when my humor had gotten to such a dark level, and I was clueless as to why it had.

Brack walked up, inspecting the fare. "Chainsaw chicken, huh? No wonder our vegetarian leader was digging through boxes for cereal."

Chortling, he decided to ditch eating for sleep. I could no longer stomach the thought of food, either, so I traded my empty cardboard dishware for a few extra minutes of rest too. The instant I stepped out of the cool, upper 90-degree shack into the 120-degree heat, my hunger disappeared.

\* \* \*

As we got further and further into our deployment, humor became the main coping method for many people in my unit. I think we all knew this to some extent. I probably should've questioned myself when I began finding my own troubles and traumas so funny.

We spent the rest of that holiday weekend trying to find the missing soldier's body. Time and again we made supply runs to our teams searching the river while each day seemed to be hotter and longer than the one before. In retrospect, we should've been more excited that we found him on the last day, but I think we mostly wanted to get out of there.

On the last trip out, we had to pick up our search team, then hop over to the nearby special operations outpost, called Firebase Cobra, and retrieve a mound of gear. It was 120 degrees outside for the umpteenth day in a row, and Brack was trying to calculate the weight and balance for everything: zodiac boat, engine, random gear, and a seven-man mixed team of operators.

In other words, he had no idea how much any of this was going to weigh. One glance at the fuel gauge told me we didn't have much time left to decide, or we would be camping there.

"Hey, crew, I'll pick it up and see how high we can hover. If it's good, we'll take off over the wall at 12 o'clock." I referenced the double-stacked, wire-wrapped, earth-filled defensive wall, called hescoe barriers, 20 meters off of our nose.

"Uh, I'm seeing a solid two feet," Brack announced as confidently as 24 inches could be labeled solid.

We all agreed that was plenty to clear the wall, but I didn't know for sure, nor did I care. I couldn't speak for anyone else, but in truth, I just didn't want to be there.

So, having some power at my disposal, enough for two feet, anyway, I inched the aircraft forward. Doing everything in my power to not lose either of those feet as a tradeoff for momentum, the helicopter slowly gained speed. I half expected the wheels to bounce off the ground, but I was trying to avoid that, as that would kill velocity. Painfully, delicately, I was able to let the reins out of aircraft tail #204, putting faith in my favorite helicopter to help a brother out.

At the last second we got through translational lift, feeling the aircraft pull us airborne. We cleared the obstacle by at least both of those two feet, maybe even three, from my vantage point.

Turning south away from the small valley, the tiny firebase disappeared behind us as we climbed high enough to clear the mountain range for the last time.

* * *

Like most of my subconscious choices, I don't remember exactly when I quit caring about so many things. Pilot safety classes label this mindset as get-home-itis, the poor judgment that results from a feeling of having to get somewhere or do something. But that was supposed to apply to individual situations, not last a lifetime.

For me, *fuck it* became an easier and faster answer than consideration, trusting in the feel of things. The problem was, I couldn't trust my feelings anymore, and this change happened without me ever actually deciding to live like this. Somehow, though, it became my attitude to not care about myself, in favor of any other priority, including convenience.

I had no idea the extent to which this perspective would later impact my life, but I was slowly learning how to not care about anything.

# CHAPTER 6

# FAKE IT 'TIL YOU MAKE IT

**LAS VEGAS, NEVADA, FALL 2011**

"So you want me to pretend that life is good?" my inquiry was loaded with sarcasm.

"Pretty much." The sage advice tumbled off of another counselor's tongue.

This one, however, sounded crazy enough to make me want to listen. "Act how you want to be, and eventually life will catch up."

Following my accident, I was making my first real attempt at recovery. I had no idea how long the process would become, but that is neither here nor there.

Half a dozen sessions into therapy, I was awaiting divorce papers to sign after the long, nine-month separation. I'd quit opiates not long before, cold turkey, and was making progress toward not drinking.

It had been months, and life had finally started to calm down. I was able to spend some time with my children, not much, but some was better than none. I quit going out to bars so much, and I'd learned to take my frustrations out on my new motorcycle by going for longer and more frequent rides. For some reason, riding gave me peace.

In a strange turn of events, that peace and the little happiness I took from it resulted in something beyond memorable happening. After riding around town one frigid November evening, I stopped at a local restaurant to get out of the cold and ran into one of the gunners from my unit eating dinner.

Joining my friend, it wasn't long before life was to take a dramatic turn. Before my food had even arrived, I watched a tall, stunning blonde walk through the door. I knew before even getting past her eyes that this girl was a drop-dead knockout. To be truthful, I'm not sure I ever got beyond her eyes.

This moment became etched in my memory for some reason. I felt as if I'd known her my entire life. I even asked the friend sitting next to me who she was, convinced I'd merely forgotten her name.

Neither of us knew, though. For some inexplicable reason, that beautiful girl felt the same way and actually came up to me to find out who I was! I couldn't help but stare at her as she made her way around the bar, just as I had from the second she entered the establishment.

"Hi, I'm Jacqui." My future wife introduced herself.

"Hi, I'm Robert," I responded in kind, "and I have to be honest. I'm going through a divorce and not looking to meet anyone right now."

My words made a futile attempt at sticking to my plans to remain single, while my eyes told her the exact opposite.

"Well, I live in Minneapolis, and I'm leaving tomorrow morning, so I'm in the same boat." She laughed.

I offered her a seat, as my feeling of *knowing* grew stronger. We spent the rest of the night smiling, talking, and getting to know each other. I couldn't believe how every cell in my body seemed to recognize this woman.

The platonic night continued as we went to her family's house, but neither of us wanted it to end there. We didn't finish our discussion until five in the morning. That was short-lived, however, as I returned a few hours later to drive her and her friends to the airport.

Every day, I left my meaningless desk job and went straight home to make it in time for our webcam dates. Each night we spoke for hours, usually until at least three in the morning. I hung on her every word and listened like I hadn't listened to anyone since leaving my crew. I also opened up like I never had before. In less than a month, she was a Las Vegas resident.

Now, I'm not going to sit here and say this relationship changed anything else for me. In fact, it probably made my life much harder in some areas. For some reason, though, the moment we met, that connection, that...whatever it was, stuck out to me. I felt as if something greater existed, that something good was still in my future.

I couldn't get that tiny feeling of knowing out of my thoughts, even if I'd wanted to. That faith wasn't the same as carrying a well-worn bible, but at this point in my life, anything was better than nothing.

\* \* \*

## LAS VEGAS, NEVADA, SPRING 2012

"Oh, my gosh, yes, you need to find out!" My counselor shared her latest advice with enthusiasm. "Do you not get it? You've got each one of those patients locked inside your head. In there they can neither live nor die, they're stuck in the helicopter, still hurt!"

Nodding, but not agreeing, I slouched across from my fellow Captain and randomly-assigned mental health counselor in her tiny office while she laid out how simple my problems were.

I was to go home that night and research which of my patients had lived or died. *Is she serious?*

My body slid further into my seat, and I took the opportunity to disengage my eyes while she turned her back and outlined my homework above the noise of information being punched into the absurdly outdated computer. Bland government carpet as thick as cardboard, and less giving, served to cover the concrete foundation in the cramped building, while providing neither comfort nor beauty.

Sighing in a manner more consistent with losing than relief, I queried, "So, how many patients do I have to do this for?"

I did not want to hear any number more than zero.

Without even spinning the chair around, her reply was, of course, "As many as possible."

The clacking on the keyboard was the only sign of life in the room for a solid minute. I didn't know if she even noticed the silence.

*Holy shit! Is she for real?* My mind again pled with me to leave, like a toddler tugging on his mother's dress.

"Okay, I will." I murmured the right answer, exactly how I'd been taught and trained.

At some point, I'd forgotten how to answer honestly and instead only knew how to give the right answer. But, to be sincere, I no longer cared either way. It didn't matter how I felt anymore.

\* \* \*

Later that evening I found myself sorting through various media, looking for clues to riddles I didn't want to solve. It went on for hours into the night. I scrolled through hundreds of articles, pictures, and stories until I saw something in an online news source I recognized. It was dated 2010.

"What the...? What is this!" I asked nobody.

*What is this picture? I know that boot!* My anger demanded answers, demanded accountability. *We trusted him!*

An Associated Press photographer, who flew with us a few times, had gained our trust and promised to never photograph Americans or our allies. That was our one golden rule. I'd just learned by accident that he'd taken pictures of our patients, in spite of this, between the helicopter and the operating room.

I felt as if someone in my family had been killed and others found it newsworthy. I wanted revenge, needed justice. I didn't care how. I didn't know it went that deep, but I touched every ounce of anger inside me that night. This wasn't the first time my emotions were translated into recklessness, but it was the first time they had a suicidal undertone.

Taking the stairs two at a time, then three, I zoomed into the garage and jumped on my Harley, with no concern for the outcome of the ride. I didn't care that I'd pancaked my last bike. I needed to get out of there.

The fact that I was usually dressed for a quick getaway made the proposition that much easier. My keys and my wallet were all that was necessary to disappear at any time.

I soon roared my motorcycle onto the highway, going full throttle the split-second I shifted into each higher gear. Highway traffic was non-existent in the Vegas suburbs after midnight, and light poles flashed past at an ever-increasing speed.

First 96, then 100, 110, 120...my speedo-tachometer was pegged, yet the highly modified bike was still pulling away.

I didn't care if my helmet shattered into a million pieces as I threw it onto the median. I didn't even bother to look back to see it land. The only thing I was sure of was my engine was heating up. I could feel it burning through my jeans, despite the cool night air and the speed.

My throttle remained full open as I begged for an end to it all. However, the funny thing about not believing in God, or anything in this life is, you get what you ask for. I believed in nothing, so nothing answered.

I don't know how long I rode, all while pleading for death, mentally and physically. When I finally got to the cheap townhouse where I rented home those days, I was exhausted. I didn't know how I was alive, but at least I no longer wanted to die. However, I wasn't sold on living, either.

I should've felt more appreciative, but I wasn't sure gratitude was possible for me at that time. Or rather, I was not in a place to discover the questions that could lead me to any sort of lasting peace. I wanted to make all of this crap go away, but I had no idea how.

Still wearing jeans, a t-shirt, and leather boots, I passed out on top of the bed for my three- to four-hour pre-nightmare nap and yet again, never wondered about or understood how to question my lifestyle choices.

\* \* \*

I gave up my search for any of my former patients after that incident. I went to my counselor and came clean about what happened. Up until that time, my medical records only listed me as having Readjustment Disorder and a brain injury. After this, however, I was issued an official PTSD diagnosis. Apparently I'd surpassed the threshold for crazy behavior, but nothing changed for me.

In fact, things got worse. In my mental health treatment, I was required to go to therapy twice a week. I switched from a cognitive-based plan (where I was supposed to convince myself of the right and wrong way to behave and why) to a treatment called Prolonged Exposure (PE).

I had my hunches about PE, but I gave it a shot, nonetheless. It turns out my fears were correct. Prolonged Exposure was just as miserable in therapy as it was in any survival situation.

I was to write about my missions, read about them, record them, and listen to those narratives throughout the day. Then I was to re-write, re-read, re-record, re-listen, and re-live them all. I did this several times a day, every day.

For months I felt, tasted, and inhaled the heat, the dust, and the death all over again. I re-lived, re-lost, and re-hated every single atrocious second of that war. I agonized over all of my choices and the path that I'd walked. I again felt pride at my successes, followed by shame and humiliation for that enjoyment. I became numb to my pain and helpless against my anger.

At work, somehow I'd become stuck in a typical staff position, doing mundane tasks as in any random government paperwork job. Originally I'd been tasked into a leadership billet and was working there while still flying. Since the motorcycle accident, however, I hadn't been allowed to fly. Now, I doubted the Air Force would ever let me back into the cockpit. On top of this, my boss was deployed, and I was supposed to be filling in as the acting commander.

So, that was the position I found myself in: acting commander of a non-flying support office that did...stuff. I had no idea about anything I did, and I didn't care. I needed much more serious mental treatment, not this repetitive cycle of staring into the past. But who would walk into their boss's office and tell him they needed to be removed from duty?

Or, in my case, I needed to call my boss's boss in a different state, whom I'd never met, and tell him I was crazy, brain damaged, and needed help.

*Better yet,* my subconscious reasoned, *I'll just drink my face off and pretend that life is awesome.*

So that's what I did. For the next six months, I lived this pattern of anxiety, anger, and depression, broken up by the highs of adrenaline, the addiction of exercise, and the euphoria of new love. It had to be, or I might not have survived.

Most of all, I suppressed everything. I hid how badly I was hurting from everyone. I lied to my counselors. I lied to myself. I lied to defend lies. Protecting anything that allowed me to cope and get my wings back was all that mattered. Somehow, this perspective transitioned into a way of life.

Nobody ever got a full picture, and I allowed no one in completely. For someone living and breathing a lifestyle of suppression, unfortunately, that was the easiest way to continue. I shut myself off to more and more family members and friends as time went by. The only people allowed to remain in my life were loyal drinking buddies.

I even tried to cut Jacqui off, more than once, sometimes more than once a week. When I was having a good day, we were madly in love. On a bad day, I wanted nothing to do with her. For the most part, nobody except Jacqui knew what was going on inside of me. And for some reason, she insisted on staying around.

My life continued this way for a time, *Faking It 'Til Making It.* The problem with that, however, was at some point I had to define what the *It* was in order to *Make It*. And for me, the last time I bothered defining anything was to label myself as a pilot who couldn't fly, a penguin, useless and outdated.

Mentally and emotionally beaten down, without a glimpse of my soul or how to rent one, I committed myself to continuing this life by suppressing every problem. This is how afraid I was of losing my job, my identity.

As far as work was concerned, this meant I was good enough to show up in uniform and wait for that medical approval to fly. Being so backed up with medical profile reviews and evaluation boards, however, the Air Force flight waiver process could literally take years.

As for what to do with a pilot who couldn't fly? Well, there were some pretty sweet locations with administrative staff positions — places like Italy, Germany, and across the Pacific.

Unfortunately, there were also non-flying staff jobs for helicopter pilots in places such as Africa, and I had signed away my vote at age 18. So, in the fall of 2012, guess where I was sent next?

\* \* \*

*Thus far, the stunning success of my mental health counseling, almost two years running, was to convince my medical and mental health providers to recommend me for a flight waiver, which was the next to last step before being allowed to fly again. A side effect of this was that I was also the perfect candidate for staff deployments, which are selected on an individual basis rather than as a unit. The Air Force rescue community had more commitments overseas for pilots than it could fill.*

*Having seemed to fulfill all the necessary requirements to keep my job, which was all I cared about achieving, it only made sense for me to be deployed solo. However, this was correct only when viewed from an outside perspective. In truth, all I had actually accomplished in mental health treatment was regaining the ability to smile professionally and say, "Yes, sir." I hadn't improved a single thing other than appearances.*

## HORN OF AFRICA, SPRING 2013

Three weeks after being returned to deployment status (but not flight status), I was picked as Director for Personnel Recovery for a Joint Task Force in the Horn of Africa.

This was a fancy way of saying I had to go sit in Africa and track every American or allied force in the nearby two million square miles of our Area of Responsibility. This meant every friendly around, from chaplains and civil engineers building schools, to teams conducting a private war against pirates/terrorists, to Western prisoners held by the enemy, some for years.

My job was to track and have or be able to provide rescue/recovery/re-integration plans for anyone and everyone. To do this, the Task Force had a small detachment of PJs, less than a bare minimum of helicopters, a C-130 airlift, along with aircrew and maintenance. The Assistant Director billet for my office went unfilled (as in, the rescue community was literally out of officers to fill it), and I had three non-commissioned officers (NCOs) to help me keep things going 24/7 (with a fourth in charge of all re-integration plans). We were absolutely undermanned for the scale of our responsibility, but that is all I can say about this job.

I reflected on these details, among other things, while sitting alone, watching the projector screen get prepared for movie night on base. Those other things on my mind were primarily the way I'd ended my last conversation with Jacqui. I felt guilty about how it ended, but despite that fact, I made no attempt to get out of my seat and call her back.

"Last night? It went great, thanks for asking," I'd lied.

*Last night's operation went terribly...* I didn't bother finishing the pointless thought or trying to start an even more meaningless sentence I wouldn't be able to complete.

My classified status meant I couldn't share much of this job with my new fiancée, so why bother saying anything? Shortly before I left for Africa, Jacqui had given birth to our baby girl. I'd made it a point to not get married just for the sake of a child, and then, of course, proposed like a love-struck idiot soon after realizing a much deeper love with the shared experience of a new child.

"I just need a beer," I had mumbled. I believed this so much that I rushed to end my conversation with this woman who was so in love with me.

"Please call me when you can, I'll be here." The support she offered was beautiful.

It was also thrown away in a hurry to get to my coping source: drinking. No, not even that thought got me up. I'd convinced myself I needed this beer, so that's what I did. I drank.

The patio used for the movie was filling up, but I sat at the edge of the scattered cheap plastic seating, hoping to avoid others.

Contemplating all that had happened there, I summed it up in another quick lie. *This has been an easy deployment.*

In truth, it was nothing more than an attempt to change the subject in my head while swatting mosquitos away. Taking a large gulp of Tusker, a favorite local Kenyan beer, I paid attention to people-watching while trying to avoid true reflections on what had actually happened on this deployment.

Though I still had no clue I was suffering complications from the effects of brain damage, it was causing me serious problems. My addictive behaviors and needs intensified as my emotional struggles manifested too often. Not long into the deployment, I'd gone through an emotional fit of frustration and punched my laptop computer in half.

After two months in humid, windowless, classified cells, I learned a painful truth. The perspective I'd slowly gained was my job was not to provide rescue support to anyone, rather, it was to document support to everyone in the AOR.

The situation wasn't that anyone was unwilling to launch rescue, if necessary. Instead, the deal with Africa was that the region was too big, and there simply wasn't enough going on - missions were intermittent at best, not happening on a regular basis. Our country lacked the resources to establish an acceptable rescue response method or timeline for most of the region; however, we also lacked the stomach to blatantly state this.

Time and distance weren't always realistic considerations, as the nation had discovered during the Benghazi fiasco. My office was called about sending our aircraft to pull out the diplomatic staff, since we were in Africa.

One of my NCOs and a good friend tried to explain Benghazi was farther away than the distance from New York to Los Angeles. To attempt a rescue in a helicopter was beyond pointless. Nevertheless, he sat there on one end of a classified phone and lived through it until nobody was left to rescue.

*But,* like I'd reasoned earlier, *it's all meaningless.*

The day before was the end of a long preparation and the start of a short operation to rescue a western hostage. There were a lot of moving parts from a lot of different places. Anticipation was high, to say the least. I'd stayed up the entire night, only to do nothing as a team member was captured.

Both hostages were then executed, live on Pred-Porn. As someone used to taking off and asking questions later, sitting on my hands watching this unfold was a new low.

I'd just left the electronic paperwork storm in my office that was the aftermath and couldn't share anything else, so even speaking about this little bit would've been a waste of time.

*...Almost as pointless as my last Afghani Scramble...* My mind taunted, trying to dig up the past.

Before taking that thought any further, I drank it away as quickly as possible. I had no desire to open Pandora's box by analyzing the connection between the previous night's operation and my final Afghani experience.

This was because I still refused to fully question my past. I felt myself disappearing again, but there was nowhere to go. I could dive into my memories like always, but that no longer helped. I felt nothing but mind-numbing emptiness, a gift from months-long devotion to exposure therapy.

That was my final determination about Afghanistan, all of my combat time, it seemed. Big, gaping holes of life lessons filled to the brim with an education I no longer wanted. I hated every memory, yet I refused to part with that hatred because it gave me identity. It protected me from everything. My anger was beyond addictive, it was beginning to control me.

This was how I subconsciously resolved to go through the rest of my life. And thanks to any impulsive behavior I could get away with, I never truly analyzed any of this.

If I'd been able to honestly evaluate myself, I might've found that my memories weren't empty and numb, it was me.

# CHAPTER 7

# ACCEPTANCE

## LAS VEGAS, NEVADA, SPRING 2013

Everybody knows someone who got married in some wild, unique, Vegas kind of way. For a lot of our friends, Jacqui and I were that couple after our wedding.

The year before, Jacqui's father lost a long battle with cancer. Diagnosed as terminal with six months left, he battled his way through another two years of life. Having spent part of that life building, repairing, and riding old Harley-Davidson motorcycles, it was only fitting that we were married on the back of my bike in a drive-thru wedding ceremony at the Little White Wedding Chapel.

Giving her away? Her Uncle drove her down the aisle on the back of her father's Harley. More than a dozen motorcycles, cars, trucks, and a limousine packed with girls wearing dresses too nice for bikes, formed a caravan down the Vegas strip with us as we ventured out on a new life together.

Many people talk about how life tends to slow down after marriage. Couples stay in more, maybe even enjoy binge-watching some TV shows while binge-eating together, silly little things like that. I don't blame them. These things are fun, cute even.

But they weren't for me, oh, no, not for us. I wasn't exactly capable of that anymore. As my ego would say, *I preferred to keep things interesting.*

My life instead became another pattern, but this time it was a repetition of suppressed emotions. I loved my new wife more than life itself. This was just an expression for most folks, but, unfortunately, it was all too true for me. The downside to that truth was I hated nearly every other part of my life, including myself.

Jacqui looked inside me and found the little joy remaining. She spent enormous amounts of time coaxing the tiniest pieces of love and laughter out of me. That was all I could manage, and for some reason, it was enough for her.

Following my tour in Africa, I switched to flying drones. On paper that is. In the military, switching career fields meant I had to wait for a training slot to open.

At work, I became a generic staff guy back in my original rescue squadron. Nearly every day I sat at the operations desk and stared at the sand-covered mountain across the helicopter parking ramp and the parallel runways. Here in Vegas it was named Sunrise Mountain, but it was similar in every appearance to the mountain range north of Khandahar Airfield. I had no idea what the actual name was; there, pilots called it Three Mile Mountain because, well, it was three miles north of the airfield. No matter the day, the view would bring up memories of the quiet time of morning just before fighting started in RC-South, or Khandahar Province.

Without a clear purpose at work, the main focus of my life became an absolute fixation on my emotions. I became a slave to my environment, as I lived in a world where I discovered more each day about my mental disorder. The problem was, I never considered myself disabled. I never saw the big picture and was left trying to interpret the small parts I saw through broken filters.

The end result? I was a disaster — a walking time-bomb. One of my daily tasks became covering up any possible trail of destruction from the day before, which usually occurred in some sort of social setting.

I coped by doing the only things I allowed myself to believe in. Trying to rid myself of stress, I started my day with ridiculous workouts, seven-to-eight mile runs or two-hour weightlifting circuits. And if I couldn't begin, or worse, finish, the entire day was stuck in the same nightmarish attitude in which I had woken up.

I drank alcohol almost every night. Motorcycles and a motorcycle club, or MC, lifestyle became the inevitable outcome. I'm certain a switch to a one-percenter, or outlaw club would've been my eventual destination, too — probably sooner rather than later. I was becoming that turned off to any part of normal society.

Riding motorcycles and drinking beer with my buddies became who I was. We often volunteered for fundraisers and enjoyed helping charities, but to be realistic, this was all another way to isolate myself. Being this way covered up the fact that I never wanted to be in public. The bike, the clothing, the exponentially increasing ink, these things were how I kept people away from me, so I never had to interact with others except on my own terms. I simply never became aware of my isolation because I was always in public.

An added benefit was I knew much more easily who might be a threat based on who was comfortable around me. The assumed relief this gave my anxiety brought no actual peace, though, as

I continued to evaluate every single person and situation for threats.

These things developed into a cycle that fed the darker side of my psyche daily through a variety of things: alcohol, motorcycles, barhopping, binge-eating, or anything that satisfied an impulse instead of facing my demons.

Regardless of the coping method of choice, arguments always ensued whenever I got uncomfortable in any situation. I had no idea I was causing these verbal fights, subconsciously taking offense at the slightest thing so I had an excuse to leave at any time.

My typical attitude was similar to a normal mindset on any other person's worst day, metaphorically doused with jet fuel and lit on fire through recklessness and hatred. That combination of energy had become my normal speaking voice, but I had no awareness of this. This caused problems for everyone else, though, and then I would end up reacting to the very behavior I'd created.

The worst part of living this way was I had no inkling of the role that I played in causing trouble for myself or my loved ones, who were forced to see and sometimes live through this cycle with me.

\* \* \*

## LAS VEGAS, NEVADA, SPRING 2013

So, how did all of this self psychoanalysis play out in real life? Well, more patterns began to emerge. Getting out of one destructive cycle of life usually meant I was entering a different, still dangerous pattern.

Just before going to Africa, I'd been thrown into handcuffs at a college football game after some random guy shouted at me about my shirt color. The fact that he was the biggest dude out of at least half a dozen and I was alone made no difference to me. The fact that a larger group of metro police stood next to them made even less of a difference.

As I charged the hostile group, all that mattered was how I felt, the stung pride that needed avenging. I made a straight run at my offender, trying to leap past his first row of friends and get at least one good punch in before they all pummeled me into oblivion. (At least, that was my split-second reaction. I didn't think any of this through very well.)

The next thing I knew, the police had me wrapped up before I landed on the ground. Thankfully, my swing had been thrown off by the attempt to dive over his buddies, and I'd missed. I probably even missed in a cartoon-ish sort of way — it was that bad.

For another half hour, I stood detained next to the group I had rushed, listening to their insults. But with every put-down, they subversively reminded Metro Police that my punch had missed, and I wasn't in the felony category. Misdemeanor was about the only positive label I had going at that moment in time.

I continued this sort of behavior into my new marriage. Two days before our wedding in May of 2013, we almost called it off. The night before, Jacqui had begged me to stay away from a bar fight. "Please don't go to jail the night before our wedding!"

Ten minutes later we walked into VIP seats to see a good friend perform the lead in a Vegas show. The dichotomy should have made me dizzy, but for some reason, this all happened so often that it had become normal for me.

Time and again, the inability to accept my emotional prison walls manifested itself physically as I tore down the actual walls or doors at home. On occasion, I would smash a plate or a coffee cup. Phones tended to the be the most expensive item, but that didn't matter as I had destroyed over a dozen of them.

Reckless behavior became a horrible pattern. Jumping out of cars was the riskiest repetitive action, by far. This also became routine, unfortunately, as my only tool for getting out of a bad situation was to run. The second I felt something coming on, I left, and being inside cars, moving or not, made no difference to me.

\* \* \*

## LAS VEGAS, NEVADA, SUMMER 2013

I don't know how anyone used to find out about random, unexpected deaths. Today, in the rescue world at least, a whisper on social media draws a private, worldwide storm as friends and family members claw for details — anything that indicates which of their loved ones were hurt or killed. The problem is, nothing can be said in the open until immediate family notification is confirmed, which usually means a day or two wait.

A friend was killed in a helicopter crash over the summer. Mark's crew did a similar thing to what I stupidly did over Khandahar Airfield, i.e. being too aggressive in a turn. The pilot didn't have the power to bank so steep, which caused the aircraft to essentially fall out of the sky. In this case, however, the pilot didn't fully level the helicopter, and they impacted at an angle.

The rest of the crew got out, but Mark was likely killed on impact. Round after round of ammunition cooked off as the aircraft burned to the ground, forcing the crew and PJs to helplessly wait. For a long time, thoughts of my own screw-up and guilt from what could've been in southern Afghanistan crept back in, well, more often than normal.

Less than five months later, in January of 2014, I found myself online for hours. It was a pitch-black night, and I was frantically posting, messaging, or reading anything I could after learning that our sister squadron in England had lost a crew. *Andy's unit...*

Sometime later that evening, I finished writing Andy's wife, Afton, begging for any details or news. *Why can't I get ahold of him?*

Looking away from the bright laptop in an otherwise dark, empty room, I felt a warm remembrance of the last time I'd spoken to Afton. It had been two years since, the winter of 2012, but she was one of those people who made it feel like yesterday. Afton was also a gunner; I usually forgot that as she'd been stuck at a desk for so long while we were stationed together.

Andy and Afton were married in the summer of 2011, right before she'd been sent overseas. He was to complete another deployment before moving to join her. At the time, I was living in Andy's apartment for a couple of months over his tour, and she'd called to ask if I could send something to her in England.

Promising anything she needed, I couldn't help messing with her, "Hey, Afton, by the way, your bed is re-eeeal comfortable."

"Damn it, Rob, you better not be having any whores in our apartment!" She could barely get the words out through her laughter.

"Actually, no...well, maybe one..." I said, jokingly leading into the excitement I felt about my future wife.

Blinking through tears, I returned my mind to the present and my eyes to the glowing screen, only to notice I still needed to hit *Send*. Immediately after posting the message, I checked out her social media page, hoping to find another friend who might have answers.

This was when the fear stopped, only to be replaced with denial. Afton's page was slowly being covered in messages as I found a truth I couldn't unsee. One posting after another was changing in content, from begging for answers to RIPs as more and more friends caught on.

*Holy shit... Afton's dead!* I had forgotten she was flying again.

Afton had been almost like a kid sister in the squadron between deployments. She'd fallen in love with and changed my friend's life during a horrible time for him.

*This doesn't make any sense...* I sat up the entire night crying and drinking, finding out the other names in the crew, then drinking and crying some more. *Chris. Sean. Dale...Jesus Christ.*

I wish I'd known that this numb, empty feeling wasn't empty at all. Something was there that cut off all sensation. And when paired with alcohol, that deep, depressing, shut-down of an emotion demanded a drinking relationship every time.

The next day, I went to work and happened upon a checkride (evaluation flight) in my drone training. I'd known about it, but in the turmoil of the previous evening had decided against any preparation and, of course, failed the ride. That part was funny to me, though, because I realized I had no desire to ever know how to work that piece of scrap. (Somehow, I crammed enough to pass the retake flight, finish my drone training in time, and attend the memorial.)

After Afton's funeral, still in shock at the death of Andy's wife and her entire crew, I had a breakdown in the Las Vegas airport when Jacqui and I were heading home. I think what upset me the most was having to pick one funeral to go to. I'd never considered anything like this before, but the memorials were spread all over the country on the same weekend.

After landing at the airport, instead of letting my wife drive us home, I dropped my wallet and phone into her lap and walked toward the Interstate, no future plans in mind. I had no idea what set me off, but all that mattered was my hate.

Unfortunately for me, I had no capacity to reflect on that then. I couldn't question anything. The only thing I could do was search for more things to be furious about.

Two miles later, as I trudged down the shoulder of the highway, I should've been worried about a lot more than I was. The assumption was I knew exactly where I was, but, in reality, I was lost in so many ways.

I had no identification, no vehicle, no wallet, no phone and could easily have been seriously hurt or killed by any number of things: cars, things being kicked up by cars, things being thrown out of cars, things being launched from the hands of drunken frat boys in cars. The list was endless.

However, anger owned me. I was addicted to it. I was sweating from the rage that controlled me, yet I had no clue why I was even supposed to be mad.

Soon, a taxi with my wife in it stopped beside me. I yelled at the driver to go away, but half a mile and five minutes later, they pulled up again. I shouted the driver away before my wife could talk me inside the cab. I was too mad. This happened again with the same result.

For an unbelievable fourth time, they tried to get me off the Interstate and into that taxi. The cabbie probably thought I'd smash his car up because I never saw him a fifth time.

A few miles later, Las Vegas Metro Police picked me up. *Should've seen that one coming...*

* * *

## LAS VEGAS, NEVADA, WINTER 2014

I finally arrived at the drone unit to which I had been reassigned, not even the least bit thrilled. I suppose my new life there was doomed from the start. I just couldn't buy into the mission. In this squadron of a couple hundred or so airmen, I believe the few people who enjoyed their jobs did so primarily because it was labeled top secret. To me, however, *classified* rhymes too much with cover-up.

Despite any and all disagreements otherwise, I have committed to uphold my oath. Therefore, I will only say that my unit supported Operation Enduring Freedom, and we killed on average 2.1 people worldwide each day.

Even though I never pulled the trigger, on my own personal level, it felt a lot like murder.

\* \* \*

## LAS VEGAS, NEVADA, SPRING 2014

Within a few months, I was in need of psychological treatment. I could've been labeled legally insane. Every erratic, emotional decision I was making was the tiny tip of a large iceberg that had become an almost daily pattern of life for me. Before long, I reached my snapping point.

In May of 2014, I walked up to my wife, fell into her lap, and broke down. "I can't live this way anymore."

The next day, I returned to the base mental health clinic, knowing this was the end of the line for me as a pilot. I wish I could say the craziness ended there, but that was not the case. I already knew my career was over, but I had no clue when the end would come. (In total, it was another 18 months before I was medically released.)

I was put to work in a windowless vault doing pointless unclassified paperwork. I proofread personnel reports daily as kill after kill was logged on paper that would never see the light of day.

It didn't even feel like I was in the military anymore. I wore a green suit and kids I didn't know called me *Sir*, but that was about the extent of familiar participation in any uniformed service. I'd never felt so helpless or hapless in my life. I was certain I was smiling properly, though.

It took almost six months for a Medical Evaluation Board to even begin my mental and physical health ratings. The Board ordered dozens of tests and exams to determine how degraded I'd become in every conceivable area. Eventually the members of this Board would be the ones who determined my VA rating, which controlled my entitlement to any post-service benefits.

This was such a long process that all it meant for me was, *Continue crying about your past every week while we ensure you are kept in as worthless a situation as possible.*

The Medical Evaluation Board was a years-long sentencing for me to stay stuck, in every possible way. I couldn't be promoted, couldn't move, couldn't quit, couldn't be used, or apparently even talked to.

My love affair with alcohol took a turn to a personal worst. And I celebrated this fact every single day. I always found a reason to party. On days I didn't have an excuse, I drank without one.

In the fall of 2014, my freedom of choice regarding alcohol came to a screeching halt. After a night of riding motorcycles around town, I went home at one in the morning. Unable to sleep yet again, I got up and ventured to a local casino, gambling into the morning.

Somehow, I kept up the hottest roll in the history of craps, and I was up thousands. At nearly five in the morning, Jacqui showed up to drive me home, but the winning continued, so we stayed. (You never quit on a heater, right?)

Entering a breakfast diner to eat after cashing out my winnings later that day, I was triggered by something...again...and left...again. Blazing hot from the rage that controlled me, I walked down the center median of the four-lane road. It's interesting to note that no matter the substance, situation, time, or cause, once the emotion took over for me, it took over unconditionally. No amount of substance or behavior could take me away from my identification with anger.

Within minutes, my wife pulled up alongside me, but this time, my hatred answered everything. When she wouldn't leave me, I picked up a cantaloupe-sized rock and smashed the rear corner panel of our SUV with it.

It turns out this was Jacqui's limit on insane behavior, and she called for backup to get me calmed down. A short six-hour chase later, I conceded to needing that assistance. My wife and two of my kids were forced to watch as I was driven away to be locked up at an in-patient mental health facility in downtown Las Vegas.

One of the hardest truths I've had to experience in life is that sometimes there are no ways to apologize, and eventually, the word *sorry* loses all meaning.

\* \* \*

## LAS VEGAS, NEVADA, FALL 2014

Following my all-inclusive lockdown, which turned out to be a Las Vegas detox and not a trauma center, like I'd been told, I made every possible effort to change my life. Strangely enough, I'd gotten along with everyone in the facility. I've never been around more honest, open, or kind people, at least, not lately. I was inspired to change, and I committed myself to leading a better life. I even tried to pray for the first time since leaving Afghanistan.

As fate would have it, two weeks into my home recovery, I blew out my knee playing indoor soccer. A collision with another player and the way I landed separated my patellar tendon from the kneecap. The recovery was estimated at six months, and my positivity turned into depression and resentment overnight.

From that point on, I went on an opiate spree. I began this entirely legal, months-long drug binge with everyone's favorite, morphine. I was only given half a dozen or so doses, but, man, was I hooked!

Next, one to two Percocet every four to six hours soon became three, then four, then six tablets every four-ish hours. Norco, Vicodin, and Oxycontin platters were main courses for most meals, or consumed randomly as a personal pill buffet throughout the day.

Big Pharma spends a lot of money on lobbyists in Congress, and during this time, I have to say thank you for my legal heroine. For that's what the painkillers I was taking a handful at a time of were: poppy flowers refined to a liquid or powder form (AKA opiates, opium, morphine, and they sure make a beautiful purple in the late Afghani springtime).

They give the same results as, are exactly as addicting as, and are no less deadly than heroine. The hypocrisy of our government to approve these drugs while denying other medicines... well, that's another story altogether.

The really funny part is, nobody ever added up all of the pharmaceuticals I was on. Daily anti-depressants, Xanax at will, sleep aids rotated for efficiency, a random horse-tranquilizer-sized thing for stress as I deemed necessary, and muscle relaxers completed my suburban-junkie-starter-kit. Simple arithmetic could've shown I was no longer capable of making these decisions for myself, but nobody ever did the math.

For the next several months, my life was consumed by depression and withdrawing from the world. In the long run, I found enough respect for myself to quit opiates cold turkey...only to replace them with an addiction to food and porn.

Every single meal became a pursuit of sugar for me, as huge portions became a constant theme, and I had long since quit caring. On another level, I became an official, addicted, down-trodden client of the multi-billion-dollar pornography industry. Strangely enough, despite all the advertisements claiming otherwise, my life got much, much worse.

My weight started out at a normal 200 pounds for my six-foot, one-inch frame. After beginning anti-depressant medication, I gained 20 pounds. On opiates, I was so stoned I hardly ate and lost the same amount of weight, despite being a proverbial couch potato all day, every day. When I was able to quit the pills, I gained 40 pounds in two months.

My knee recovery was on perpetual pause caused by mysterious, constant infections that baffled the military doctors. I went back time after time for random follow-up surgeries, 12 altogether. My social life became non-existent, and any remaining happiness or joy for life disappeared. I was a complete slave to the environment, and for as long as I could remember, my environment told me I was better off dead.

A few months of this and I went the other way with food. I quit eating, except for a small dinner at night. My weight plummeted from its highest, 250 pounds in December, to 220 by spring of 2015. Before the summer was over, my weight would plunge into the 160s.

In March 2015, I was thrilled to receive a call asking me to come in for the Medical Evaluation Board results. It had been close to a year after going in for help, so all I could think was, *Finally, the Air Force will let me out!*

My wife took me in, as I was unable to drive after nearly six months. This was to be my final, sweet release from whatever my military career had turned into.

Trying to ignore the chilly Vegas spring wind that never quit blowing, we walked into the base hospital for my appointment.

"Is anyone ever happy in hospitals?" Jacqui spun around for signs with arrows on them.

"I don't think anyone in the military is ever happy." I chortled, still unaware that what I saw was discolored by my own emotions. "Guess we can take this 'vator up?"

I pointed to the nearby set of polished aluminum doors. A few minutes and two wrong turns through a horrible cubicle-maze later, we sat down in a tiny office, nervous and hopeful.

The Veterans Affairs representative, an older, white-haired veteran, had been handling the VA side of things. He was short, spry, and everything his "military" counterpart, the AF medical liaison, was not. Civilian clothes or not, his exaggerated, almost celebrated, lisp and obvious unfamiliarity with acronyms outed him instantly as a temporary civilian secretary.

The VA representative welcomed us and grumbled through his obligatory speech. "This isn't final, these are only the informal results. You have the right to blah, blah, blah..."

Actually, my memory might be hazy on what my rights were. In truth, I only wanted to leave.

Next, my fifth medical liaison officer started reading the results, "So...the VA has rated you with non-combat PTSD at..."

His voice trailed off as I stared at him in disbelief.

"Non-combat?" I questioned.

"Hang on. Let me finish," the temp stated, his dramatic comeback suddenly louder than his cologne-soaked plaid shirt. "You're just a drone pilot, that's not considered combat."

"Mother—" I cut my scream short in the tight office.

Choosing to not be locked up on base instead of hitting him, I bolted out the door, heedless of the harmful effects to my most recent surgery.

I grabbed the hospital wall railing to get out of this maze faster. *How could the VA give me a non-combat rating? How could I get PTSD from non-combat...during combat!* I angrily screamed inside my head.

The next hour was a blur. Jacqui finally talked me back into the meeting so we could finish and leave.

"They must not have read your file." The VA rep scratched his head, searching for sympathy. "You'll have to go to the formal Board and appeal in person." He then went into detail about how I was to be assigned an attorney and needed to appear at a legal hearing to plead my case.

*How could the Medical Board not read my file?* I repeated these words over and over in my head. *I have a lawyer? I have to go to court to prove my service? Can't the government read the file they already have? Can't they let me out?...*

Staring into the void that was to be my near future, I must've triggered something in the VA representative's head that made him think that what he said next was a good idea.

"Now, you watch him closely." The old man leaned toward Jacqui. "Ten guys in this medical review process kill themselves every month, and five a month go to jail. I got two locked up downtown right now, and their families will get nothing, no benefits."

It was now Jacqui's turn to stare open-mouthed at the two men in disbelief. *What just happened?*

* * *

## LAS VEGAS, NEVADA, SPRING 2015

The first phone call with my lawyer was so confusing it was almost comical. I needed to gather evidence to prove I'd served overseas in the military, including personal narratives and witness accounts or descriptions of the times and places where I'd been in combat. All of my records were submitted months ago, I couldn't understand what else I could prove if those weren't enough. The shame was unbearable.

I attempted to write narratives of our missions but often locked myself away as the efforts became obsessive, with obtrusive thoughts lasting hours or even days. The nightmares, the crying fits, and the shameful, depressed retreats into myself intensified. I frequently didn't eat for multiple days in a row. I found that turning off any care for myself and the outside world was the one answer to get me out of the days- or weeks-long depressive moods.

About a month after my legal teleconference, I lost it at the base gym, crying in a bathroom stall, unable to stop re-living the hell of the narratives and my missions. The mind-traps of thought simply wouldn't shut off. And, I still needed to document more accounts of my experiences during war to provide extra proof.

That day, I had to call Jacqui to come and pick me up. I'd been driving for one week after the latest surgery, but mentally speaking, I was unable to start the car. I'd been phoning and e-mailing my mental health doctor, my lawyer, the medical liaison officer, and the VA rep for weeks, asking for help, because I was unable to live through this process anymore.

Not one of them wrote back or returned my messages. I never even heard back from my attorney. I was assigned a different one the day before my hearing, months later. (After the fact, I learned there were more than 4,000 clients congesting the Air Force medical evaluation system and only eight attorneys.)

Later that spring of 2015, I was invited to my old helicopter squadron to talk about how the crews might work in conjunction with drones, what limitations the aircraft have, and other such things. I was no longer flying but was still more than qualified to speak on the capabilities, so I obliged.

A friend I used to fly with, Dan, was there, working the same operations desk I'd been stuck at for months. Being lost in my own world and troubles for so long, I'd forgotten Dan wasn't flying. I was shocked that I'd overlooked why, and what it all must've meant for him. I was even more dismayed at the changes in him since the incident.

Dan had made a horrible mistake overseas, accidentally firing his rifle while unloading it. For as long as the Air Force was taking with my medical evaluation, they were taking even longer making sure he could never forget that split-second mistake. I'd forgotten all of this until seeing him brought it back.

Dan was one of those guys who always seemed to be up to something. If you were lucky, ridiculous pictures shared with the world were the worst consequence of his shenanigans. I can't remember a single day when he didn't have a devilish grin on his face, almost always setting a friend up in some kind of practical joke. But Dan never did so out of spite, never did it without making sure that even the victim was laughing.

I could be wrong, but I'm quite certain his most important daily concern was making others smile. Dan, or D-Sway as a lot of us knew him, was a well-liked Veteran of Afghanistan and Africa. Later on, I'd regret not speaking of the look I saw, or rather, the lack of spirit in him. His relaxed Carolina attitude had been replaced with something else, something that seemed empty but wasn't.

Eight days later, in May of 2015, Dan typed a simple post on social media: *This isn't me. This isn't my life.*

He then picked up a handgun and pulled the trigger.

*How could someone who saved the lives of 41 people hate himself that much?* I didn't understand any of what was going on around me.

I retreated into myself like never before, and I quit everything. I mean, every single thing. Before long, Jacqui started showing signs of fatigue from trying to put up with me being in her life. For some reason, she was still in love with me, but my baggage was becoming too much. The ways I had either betrayed her trust or avoided dealing with my own problems were just coming to light.

She realized my actions had turned her into an enabler, and that our party lifestyle was a cover for pain. She was untrained and unable to handle living 24/7 with someone who had a mental disorder, brain damage, and addictive issues. The emotional toll was exhausting.

A week after Dan's memorial, Jacqui had a nervous breakdown and went to the base hospital ER for help. She'd tried a different tactic initially, but after calling the Veteran Crisis Helpline, she was transferred three times and then sent to voicemail.

It took weeks before I went out into public again. We moved into the most private part of town we could find, told almost no one where we were going, and asked only one friend to help us move. Once things were in place, I made up my mind to not leave for any reason.

It wasn't until my formal medical hearing in July of 2015 that I actually left the house of my own free will, although technically I didn't choose to do this. I didn't even bother going to my squadron office to pick up travel orders, an easy paperwork requirement to journey on the government's dime. Following the trip, I never went in to file a voucher to collect reimbursement for the trip, either.

Plane tickets for two, three nights on the San Antonio Riverwalk, and all meals paid for. That is, if I could've gone into work and filed that paperwork. But I was so disillusioned and so detached from life that I wanted nothing to do with anyone else. In this aspect, I was lucky I'd had so many surgical excuses from work that nobody bothered checking on me.

Major or not, I quit...on the military, on life, on all of it. It was a miracle I'd even packed a uniform for the trip.

My new attorney, an angel disguised as a Lieutenant Colonel, greeted me with sincerity and cold-hearted bluntness. "Dude, your entire record was scanned and sent upside down. Literally, every page was upside down. I talked to the Board; no one ever read this."

I was stunned. The digital file had to be rotated one page at a time, and the Medical Evaluation Board was so overtasked that the members could allocate maybe 30 seconds to each file. I sat in silence, listening to this pitiful explanation. As had become my norm, I was uncomfortable being around...anyone. This sounds bizarre, but I was becoming uneasy even participating in conversations.

*What the—?...That temp must've scanned it in wrong!... My file was upside down, and nobody bothered to fix it? Or read it?* My gut rolled with one unexpressed emotion after another. *Fucking pencil-pushing bean counters...*

I was tasked with going through my records and selecting photos or statements that would allow changes to be made. A kind manager at a local office supply store helped me sift through hundreds of digital files from Afghanistan to compile my exhibits. I felt horrible that she was exposed to those things. My old crew, now scattered across the country, came through for me in an hour with statements. Jacqui had called them when I was too ashamed.

Within hours, the overwhelming evidence I'd supplied in defense of my own service corrected the one thing I'd challenged, combat veteran. I hadn't bothered to correct the percentage of benefits, as I was not at all concerned with fighting for extra money. I couldn't have cared less if I spent the rest of my life living under a highway overpass.

Despite everything, three nights, thousands of dollars that I would not be reimbursed for, and one and a half meals eaten between Jacqui and me, we arrived home safely. I should've been relieved, but I sunk further into depression. Everything I was, everything I had ever been, was now gone. The only thing left to do was wait for the funeral to this lifestyle.

Not knowing how to move forward, I sat indoors day after day and stared at nothing: the wall, the ceiling, the ceiling fan, whatever. Regardless of outside help or motivation offered, I was unable to get out of my personal prison.

\* \* \*

## LAS VEGAS, NEVADA, SUMMER 2015

"Nobody cares, man." My counselor, a former Marine, never minced words. "That's what each of us has to learn. It really is financially better for the government if you die, and nobody will actually care."

I'd heard this line hundreds of times by now, but each time it cut deep. I'd been told this so much that I'd developed that same laissez-faire attitude about my own wellbeing. I was unable to question my attitude that hating myself made me tougher and less vulnerable to the outside world. Every morning, my first thought was pure resentment at being awake.

*Nobody cares now, just like they didn't care before.* I wish I'd known this lesson from the start, before I tricked myself into serving in the military.

I walked outside to my truck, armed with more lessons from another therapist about how to not be miserable. Nobody seemed to know how to be happy, though.

*Twenty-two Veterans commit suicide each day.* The number played through my mind as I pulled myself up from the running boards I'd installed on the truck, in some feeble attempt to buy happiness.

*And all anyone ever says is the government wants you to quit in this process. What a joke. How do they not see they're causing it all? The government systems themselves are creating a suicide epidemic.* The futility of questioning woke me up as I recognized my change in temperament.

It took five years for me to learn how to recognize my emotional swings. Those changes could trigger a downward spiral that could last for hours, days, or weeks. It was best to stay inside during those times. Going out caused too many problems, and all of the people I met out there seemed to bother me somehow.

The last time I went out for non-medical appointments was more than two months before. I didn't expect to have any problems at a charity event, but I suppose I should've accepted the fact that I didn't fit in anywhere anymore.

Feeling the heat from my neck up to my hair, I realized I was blushing from the shame. A friend's wife had misunderstood my anxiety attack, thinking she'd offended me.

*Why'd she have to touch me?* I almost lost it again at the thought. *I don't even drink anymore and that happened...*

*It's been almost five years since Afghanistan. Five years. Why does it still feel like yesterday? Why is there no point to anything?* One of the most damaging things about not believing in God was that the complaining did nothing but tear me down. And the demolition phase, five years running, wasn't over yet.

Earlier that day, Jacqui asked me to travel to California with her to stay at a friend's place, then attend a family reunion dinner with her relatives the following night. The question would normally make me anxious, almost angry, but in spite of that, I was considering it.

The silence of my truck cab was almost deafening, the repetitive clicking of the blinker kept pointing out. So many of the Las Vegas highlights that had once attracted me now stood out for opposite reasons. Lights, sound, beer, women, party, fun, lies. I no longer wanted to know how much I could get, who I could be, how I could make myself feel like a winner instantly. It was all fake.

Somehow, I made it home without getting any angrier at the artificial scenery, although a thought dawned on me as I parked in the driveway. *I don't want any of this anymore.*

I didn't mean this from a giving up on life standpoint, not at that moment, anyway. I just needed to get out of there.

*Okay, then, I guess it's time for some California love.*

\* \* \*

## MIDDLE OF VENTURA BOULEVARD, LOS ANGELES, SUMMER 2015

A car blared its horn mere feet behind and passed, unbelievably missing me. I should've been more frightened than I was.

Oddly enough, I wasn't scared at all. I no longer even felt upset, I was confused.

I knew where I was, sure. It was hard to forget walking out into the middle of Ventura Boulevard trying to kill myself. As if to emphasize that fact, more horns screamed out as cars zipped by. It was surprising that no tires had squealed. Even more strange, nothing hit me.

This was all a simple misunderstanding. That's how these situations always started. But for me, my ability to reason was gone.

Earlier that day and the entire previous day, I'd been completely fine. I'd driven my family out to southern California to stay with a friend for his son's birthday party on Saturday, followed by a family reunion dinner on Sunday. Due to a simple mix-up in dates, we'd discovered the friend's birthday party was on Sunday night, the same time as the family dinner.

Anxiety from trying to attend both events led to being late, and misunderstandings from hurried communications led to hurt feelings. That was how easily, and stupidly, these things could begin for me.

Unfortunately, as I've already stated, my emotional need to get away trumped everything else. Cognitive abilities had gone AWOL and family ties were history.

Two college-aged kids approached me, trying to offer help as I stood behind a building, attempting to hide. However, the rage that surged through me didn't allow for sense, reason, or even a stranger's kindness.

Getting away from them, I found the sidewalk and began walking, to wherever...the beach maybe? I had a sudden urge to become a bum and live homeless and nameless for the rest of my life. I'd had the same feeling at least a dozen times that summer.

Suddenly, a car pulled up in front of me, cutting off my path and ripping me away from my daydream.

Jacqui had circled around for 15 minutes, hoping to talk some sense into me. She cut me off at the driveway of a business, in an attempt to lure me into the car before anything bad happened. Unfortunately for me, that set me off worse, and I stepped off of the curb.

"Robert!" Jacqui begged out the window in confusion and futility.

Having given into madness and being incapable of listening, I strode into traffic to kill myself, more committed with every step. I actually smiled, wondering when the fatal hit would come.

I don't know how to explain this adequately, but I suddenly felt Jacqui's mother next to me, right there in the middle of Ventura Boulevard. She was born in Simi Valley, California but had passed away five years before. I'd never even met her. But I felt her next to me just the same.

I'd expected to feel the SUV I saw coming at me, blaring its horn in disbelief. I don't know what happened to that SUV. I don't know what happened to me stopping and standing in the middle of the traffic lane, four feet from the double yellow line. To put it plainly, I was in the road...and then I wasn't.

I found myself on the opposite curb, confused, yet completely calm and aware, simply wondering, *What was that?*

I could barely piece a thought together; I was that unclear about what had happened. My wife pulled up alongside me, looking as puzzled as I felt.

Still freaked out, she begged me, "Will you please get in?"

No longer upset, I collapsed into the car. Strangely enough, although I was perplexed, I felt fine. We sat in the car for a moment, quiet and still, before Jacqui finally asked, "What was that?"

"I don't know..." I tried but couldn't understand. My brain felt lost as I tried to make sense of the thoughts running wild in my mind. *We're all dead no matter what.*

A strange déjà vu-type feeling I hadn't felt in a while hit me from somewhere deep, a place where I hid my Afghani memories. *Wait, when did I think that? Did I say that today or...*

"Please, what was that? Can I get you somewhere safe, *please!*" Jacqui's voice trembled as she white-knuckled the steering wheel.

I couldn't answer. I was stuck trying to find a lost memory, something I hadn't thought of since...when?

"We're all dead no matter what we do," I muttered. I kept thinking about that over and over but couldn't place it until...

"Oh, God, I remember." I voiced the thought, louder than intended.

"You remember what?" Jacqui asked.

\* \* \*

*By this point in dealing with a mental disorder, I had gone through many patterns of life. At first, I'd cut off anyone I assumed was the cause of my distress. Next, I transitioned to an alcoholic, then became a closet addict of legal-ish drugs or impulsive behaviors in order to quash my unaddressed problems.*

*Despite adding a brain injury, among other things, I continued fighting to get back to an undefined normal life without addressing my issues. This forced a pattern of suppression and associated explosive reactions on an unknown and irregular basis, occasionally drawing up hidden memories. The one true way to escape these patterns was to separate the memories from the lessons learned.*

*So the question becomes, at what point did I personalize these experiences to the extent that those lessons became such destructive perspectives?*

## CAMP BASTION, AFGHANISTAN, SUMMER 2010

*Squelch...*

The FM radio chirped its sole warning before a *Scramble* order to the helicopters.

Asleep in our alert tent on the west side of the Helmand River Valley, I sprang out of my short-lived rest toward the early desert morning. Everything I needed was either with me or already in the helicopter...

"Maintenance 1, Maintenance 2, can you get the cart out to tail #204?" The hand-held radio, or brick, blurted out in an incredibly delayed manner.

This woke me up to the fact that we were *not* being scrambled into action. I found myself trying to sprint through the middle of the PEDRO alert tent, looking like a jackass. Six of my closest friends were dying laughing at the scenario.

"Mother—" I cut the expletive off, compelled to join in the fun at my expense.

Andy had almost fallen out of his chair onto the plywood floor, he was choking so hard on his laughter.

*Hope they enjoyed the entertainment!* I realized there was yet again no way out of this.

"That TSD's a bitch..." My face was beet red as I collapsed into a dusty seat, uttering the only excuse I could come up with.

Brack laughed even harder, enjoying the use of his favorite acronym (he was right, though, technically you cannot say *post-*traumatic stress until you are actually post, or home).

"Fuck these flies!" Andy swatted around his face, thankfully changing the subject.

This was a much-repeated mutual feeling among all of us. The alert tent was a breeding ground for flies, more so daily because of food that got left out every time a *Scramble* was called.

"Aw, you need a backrub?" Our wingman's gunner had an easygoing southern drawl that casually hid two decades of special operations and combat rescue experience.

"What I need is to put my skin on your skin, motherfucker," Andy responded as a true gunner would.

I smiled, closed my eyes, and half-heartedly attempted to swat away a couple of flies. Folding my arms, I listened to Brack join the bickering, sounding like kids. We argued and messed around for no reason other than to have something to do.

With a 1 a.m. show time, we posted gear in the aircraft and got briefed until 2:30. After that, the eight of us in both crews piled into the alert tent, usually for some early morning poker. Dee always buried her face in a book near the Operations Desk as soon as the money broke out, so most of the time, it was six or seven of us. We rarely got scrambled at that time of day, so it had become our zen time. This time belonged to us.

Cards, and that moment of peace, only lasted for an hour or two tops, unfortunately. Everyone always got sick of the winner's gloating, and double-or-nothing offers were mostly responded to with demands for sexual favors. This meant, until our first sortie, we had nothing to do but amuse ourselves at each other's expense.

But every day, no matter how funny the jokes were, no matter how much I won or lost, anxiety built as time passed. Sometimes, we got early morning sorties. Maybe a couple of times per week on average we'd launch before sunrise. Missions hit sporadically at first, and from then on we normally weren't finished until our replacements took over at 2 p.m. (1400 hours). However, many days found us out flying until 4 p.m. (1600).

Shift times were more like suggestions for scheduling purposes. Retrieving the patient was all that mattered, and whichever crew was better prepped at shift change was the one that went out.

We had one mission where all but one crew member on the following shift had swapped flight gear when the call came. Our crew took the aircraft back, though, because we were damned if any of us would fly without all of us.

"Oh, you got jokes now, too." Andy was getting defensive about whatever Brack was accusing him of this time. "All right, motherfuckers, see what happens..."

I couldn't help but smile as I swatted more flies away, losing my battle with sleep. These guys would keep me laughing for days, but running for months on a handful of hours of sleep each night had caught up with me. I was no longer capable of resisting any available naps, no matter how short they might be. The noise faded away as my body became warm and floated toward letting go, toward relaxing, toward...

*Squelch...*

"*Scramble, Scramble, Scramble. All PEDROS Scramble!*" Every brick in the tent ordered us to the aircraft.

The tent cleared instantaneously, each crew member sprinting toward wherever they were needed.

*Thud, thud, thud, thud...*

My tan boots on the metal grates soon fell into step with the fully automatic firing of my heartbeat. My breath matched the beat of my steps soon after.

I sped up, halfway to the helicopter, almost catching up to Andy. Maintenance airmen ran from the hanger across the pads, some of the crew chiefs already stripping safety plugs and static-electric grounding lines from the aircraft. Smoke rose over the 15-foot concrete barriers surrounding us, showing the entire FOB where the trash burned all day, every day. The unnatural ash and filth choked the air being sucked into our lungs on this 400-meter dash.

A few more steps, and we were to our seats. The body armor was almost as heavy as it was burning hot. Porcelain hard armor plating, soft armor padding, seven fully-loaded searing metal magazines of 5.56 caliber rifle ammunition, another three of nine-millimeter pistol bullets, all toasting in the brownish-orange Afghani haze.

*Faster.* I pushed myself angrily, as I realized that for some reason I'd started to put my left glove on before my helmet. Doing anything out of sequence made me slower.

I threw the helmet on, last this time, as I jumped into the bird, glad now to have the glove on since the metal of the cockpit was just below a good frying pan temperature. My hands flew all over the cockpit, throwing switches, turning wafer dials, and getting the gyros spinning. Running everything through memory, the sequence had been timed out to the second.

I paid no attention to the thick dust hanging over us. We had more than enough visibility to launch the flight that day, despite how orange everything looked.

"Gunner's up," Andy announced.

"FE is up." Brack was set.

"PEDRO 24 is ready." Our wingman notified us.

"MOM, send it for PEDRO," I called out in sequence.

Stepping off the floor mic switch, I waited to copy down information about where we were headed and why. Our routine definitely had a rhythm all its own.

"PEDRO 23 Flight, stand by for MIST. Be advised, TRICKY was tasked instead." Our radio operator at MOM shut us down before we could get started.

The operations center informed us the British rescue helicopter squadron, the only other helicopter rescue unit in Helmand Province, had been assigned the mission. For some reason, our back-enders had jokingly labeled these types of *Scrambles*, getting Tricky-fucked (in honor of the Brit unit's callsign, TRICKY).

"Copy, TRICKY..." I responded to MOM, drawing the callsign out for my crew.

"...fucked!" Andy finished for me, keeping the inside joke to our intercom and off the radio.

This pattern of events happened often, sometimes more than once a day. Every time anyone in the theater needed to be medically evacuated, we ran, assuming each time it was for real. And then we waited.

Similar to what could happen at any stateside airport, sometimes the other aircraft had maintenance issues. Sometimes, the other helicopter units arrived on-scene and said no. They had the right to call things as they saw necessary. When the LZ was declared hot, they had to report it to the chain of command. And when that happened, the mission would inevitably be retasked to us.

I suppose this was what made our unit different, in the end. We would lie to go, and our crew had been forced to do that, more than once.

Under the dust we waited, yet again, as Andy had so articulately described it. "Tricky-fucked."

* * *

### HELMAND PROVINCE, AFGHANISTAN, FALL 2010
*(Two months later, following my last combat flight in Afghanistan, documented in Chapter 2.)*

"I don't think I liked that mission..." Andy finally spoke up.

Brack had walked away with the maintenance crew chief, and Dee was taking care of the required reporting with our intelligence officer. Andy and I stood with the aircraft, attempting to enjoy our victory chew and waiting on the guys from weapons maintenance, immediately after my (yet-to-be-realized) final combat mission.

I had no idea what to say. I should've told Andy what I'd seen and thought about Brack being killed on the last sortie, but for some reason, I made a stupid joke instead.

Avoiding eye contact, I spit into the sand. "Yeah well, none of this will matter when we're famous rock stars..."

I loved listening to my friend laugh, but, still, I should've said something. I felt that flight messing with me, deep down. I knew Brack wasn't dead, but for some reason I kept looking around to make sure he was still alive.

A second later our fun was cut short once again by our nemesis: the radio.

*Squelch...*

"*Scramble, Scramble, Scramble. All PEDROS Scramble!*" MOM'S operator sent the order over our closed radio network.

Taking advantage of the extra time we had, already being at the helicopter, I leaned inside and took things out of sequence, flipping switches and getting the radios up first while I slung on my armored vest and helmet.

"MOM, PEDRO 23 is still up comms, ready to copy," I replied through our aircraft radio.

"Copy 23, looks like TRICKY this time," our operator at MOM came back.

"Copy, TRICKY..." I emphasized the callsign, but mostly for the added benefit of slowing Andy down, who hadn't put his helmet on yet.

*Too late.* I saw a wad of chew already flying out past Andy's cannon barrel.

I knew our gunner was pissed, and for some reason, the fact that he saw me laugh at him for it made this moment just a little better for my friend.

"FE is up." Brack hooked into the helicopter comms with us.

"And old." Andy finished on cue.

His body language told Brack everything. "TRICKY-fuck?"

We both nodded confirmation as I finished the pilot checklists. Our aircraft couldn't use gas until being officially assigned the mission, otherwise we'd risk running out. Completing every checklist step up to Engine Start was the farthest we could go right now.

"PEDRO 23 Flight, MIST as follows: one Cat Alpha, gunshot wound, headshot, blood pressure..." Our operator cut in again.

*Fuck this!* The MIST report that I copied down was a Marine with a gunshot wound to the head, and his vitals were dropping.

"MOM, we can be off the ground in five. This dude is 15 mikes away. Request permission to launch." I demanded that we be allowed to go instead of TRICKY.

My right foot had mashed the floor mic switch, as I was using both hands to strap my harness on and throw any other switch I could. My eyes ran over everything again, hoping to steal another second from somewhere. My pleas may have been useless, but it was infuriating sometimes how slow TRICKY could be.

Nothing against the Brit helicopter aircrews, but they flew an aircraft that took much longer to start and takeoff. We were faster and had recently gotten over the hurdles of adding a refrigeration unit to the helicopter cabin. This was required to push blood to patients, rather than saline solution, which needed no cooling. The difference could be life-saving minutes. There was no longer a reasonable argument for us not being assigned this mission first.

"Copy PEDRO, stand by," our operations staff officer answered this time.

Dee jogged out from the TOC during this discussion. Her humor from earlier had disappeared. *Similar to the rest of us.*

I back-briefed her on my request to the folks at MOM as soon as she was plugged into the intercom. As I'd assumed, she was ready to go.

"Yeah, why don't we just take off?" Andy joined in the complaints. "Seriously, what are the they going to do? The patient's a U.S. Marine, and TRICKY takes for-fucking-ever!"

Soon, our PJ team joined in the conversation, and we all sat there, stating our case to each other, complaining our frustrations away as even more anxiety filled the void in their place. Still, the minutes ticked by.

"PEDRO 23 flight, request is denied. Continue to stand by." The door of futility was slammed shut on us.

*Fuck!* I knew we were right.

Nobody said anything else, though. There was no point, nothing to add. We had the entire flight route memorized. I could visualize the patient being loaded, how I'd take off over the FOB's double-stacked hescoe barriers.

Ten minutes turned into 20, then became 30. I quit counting after that. I needed more of a break after our last mission. Sweat ran down my face. I was relieved that this *Scramble* was about to come to an end soon.

*Even in October, hell is hot!* I tried switching thoughts but was unsuccessful.

Nearly an hour after the call, we saw TRICKY, the British medevac helicopter, and its accompanying Apache gunship take off.

"PEDRO 23 flight stand down," Our MOM operator called.

"Finally!" We all breathed a collective sigh of relief.

"...Patient is VSA." The operator finished the sentence in the worst way.

*Jesus.* We all thought and felt it in unison.

VSA: vital signs absent. Relief came too soon and in the wrong manner. The heat beat down on us as we sat in silence.

*We could have been there half an hour ago!* I wished someone could've explained that the pain I felt was the last shred of my soul as it tore loose and fled the scene.

*We should have taken off. What could anyone have done to us? We're all going to die, anyway.* I do not know if I said this aloud.

I leaned forward and ran these thoughts through my head. Rubbing the top of my helmet, I felt the warmth of it through the leather glove. I don't know why I did this. It's not as if I could feel anything like rubbing my actual skull. Yet for some reason I sat there a bit longer, my hands doing whatever random activity kept them from the fear of doing nothing.

I didn't hear Brack calling for the aircraft cocking checklist, which would set the aircraft for the next mission, possibly coming up any second.

*What if we had just gone?...* This thought took over my mind, while my heart hated anyone and everyone for this outcome.

"Hey, Rob, I'll get the aircraft set if you want to chill." Dee offered kindly.

Rather, it would have been kind if I had acknowledged her. Instead, I sat there and retreated into myself, sealing the prison doors with one tiny bit of reason at a time.

*Thirty minutes ago, with blood... What the hell are we doing here? Hearts and minds... Fuck their hearts and minds. What's the point to any of this?... We're all dead no matter what...* I burned these thoughts into my brain over and over.

I hated the futility of it all. I hated myself. Hate became my answer for everything. *I. Hate. My. Life.*

For yet some other unknown reason, I didn't remember taking off my combat gear for the last time. My next memory was of the conversation when I was told out of the blue that the docs thought my baby boy had leukemia.

In between that and the next *Scramble*, Dee found me collapsed in a heap on the metal grates, satellite-phone cast to the side. Even though she was half my size, somehow, Dee got me up and inside, where our boss coordinated my flight back to the U.S. around midnight. After all, we had only a short time left in Afghanistan, and my replacement was on the way.

Their logic to send me home was solid, no doubt about it. But that couldn't stop my heart from being ripped out; I had to repeatedly watch the rest of the day as my crew launched without me. They ran to the unknown while our maintenance airmen helped get the gray aircraft off the ground in minutes, every time.

Watching them take off and staring at the swirling powder, I felt alone for the first time that I remembered. I decided to follow our head crew chief's example and walk behind the maintenance hanger, lovingly called the Clamshell (because it looked like a gigantic clam sticking out of the earth).

I stood there for a minute, then collapsed to the blazing sand, and I cried. Isolated on a 90-degree autumn afternoon, I became paralyzed in ice-cold fear. This, it seems, was the sum of my lessons with which I left Afghanistan: a perspective of anger, covering up experiences of pain and loss.

To be honest, I have felt alone and afraid ever since.

# CHAPTER 8

# LETTING GO

**LAS VEGAS, NEVADA, FALL 2015**
*...continued from Chapter 1...*

C LACK!

My pistol made a loud metal thunk. Dry-fire.

"What the—" Pausing in the middle of attempting to kill myself, I opened my eyes to the present.

Years of memories had just gone through me, the waves coming in as heavy as they were fast. I ran my gaze down the open gun safe, over the corner of junk in this useless room.

I was indeed back in the moment, mentally returned to our Las Vegas house from whatever that experience was. But I no longer knew what I wanted.

*Who emptied my gun?* I was slow to ask this question, having just loaded all of them after going shooting a couple of weeks ago.

Feeling disconnected, almost detached, I peered down to my hands, now on autopilot, as they kept running through the motions. Holding the pistol in my left hand, my damaged right hand had gingerly lifted a full magazine off the gray-carpeted shelf and slid it into place. The 1911 was on standby, waiting for me to drop the slide release, which would load a .45 caliber hollow point bullet.

*That Others May Live.* I had no idea why I stopped to read this motto again.

It stood out to me, though, almost a vision of something else, a part of me I'd forgotten. I felt odd reading the laser-etched inscription on the pistol's right side one last time.

*Thunk.*

*What the hell?* My hands, still running on auto, had dropped the slide release on the gun's left side. *But it jammed? What's going on?*

I was numb, not angry. My concrete plan melted into fog and confusion while cradling the malfunctioned weapon in front of my home safe. It had a half-loaded round wedged partly into the barrel, and I no longer trusted the pistol to fire.

I stood for another second, unaware of the emptiness surrounding me. Dumbfounded, I swapped the gun for Jacqui's Glock M19, a reliable 9mm pistol.

*That's so disrespectful.* The notion appeared like a flash.

The weapon had belonged to her father before he passed away from cancer three years ago. I had no clue what to make of this feeling, when something else, something inside me, finally took over.

*What the hell are you doing?* I screamed in my head, dropping the weapon back into the safe. Running upstairs, literally to save my own life, I grabbed my phone, cursing the pain but not caring, as I gripped the banister on my way up. I texted:

> Need you to come get my guns. Safe's open. I'm
> locked upstairs. Don't talk to me.

Only a true friend wouldn't freak out upon reading this text, but it turned out I'd ignored the one positive thing going for me. More people than I would admit still cared. I heard no noise whatsoever, but in less than an hour, every single round and weapon had been cleaned out of the house. I know, I checked on my way out the door, not too long after the feat was completed.

I had no idea where I was going or what I was doing as I climbed into my lifted white Ram truck. All I knew was the combination of smashing my right hand and having a manual transmission sucked.

"Stupid stick!" I exclaimed, leaning my body over so I could use my left hand to shift the big diesel into second gear.

Rounding the corner out of the manicured fake desert landscaping that marked all Vegas suburbs, I had another weird realization. *I should go to the hospital.*

That feeling stuck out as shifting to fourth gear convinced me it was right. Fifteen minutes later, I found myself in a sparse waiting area in the hospital emergency room. The usual crowd of the unwilling, wearing a strong combination of fear, impatience, and worry, sat looking for distractions.

After giving my name to the lady at the desk, I found a seat next to the kids' play area. I had no idea why I didn't choose my usual kind of spot, safely against a wall away from others, but for some reason, I think it made me laugh.

Before long, however, the *Why* questions couldn't be put off. *Why didn't I die? Why did my gun jam? Why was it unloaded? Why did my friend want to go shooting? Why did I even respond to him? I never call or write anyone back, not anymore...*

For almost half a year now, I'd avoided answering the phone, had hardly responded to texts, and I deleted my single social media account the day after an old friend reached out for the first time in more than 13 years. Wanting to stay with a good friend instead of doing the Vegas-thing for a bachelor weekend, he actually preferred to go shooting in the desert.

*That was almost two weeks ago... Lucky timing.* This was about as close as I could get to feeling grateful or acknowledging divine influence.

*I have friends like that left?* Another quiet feeling whispered something I hadn't felt worthy of for quite some time: positive affirmation.

This emotion was strange, but it led me down a different path of questioning. *Where are these feelings coming from? What was it I felt on Ventura Boulevard? Why am I living this way? Why do I want any of this?*

"John?" Hearing my first name, which only gets used for appointments, I stood and walked toward the in-processing counter.

I almost chuckled at whether or not I'd be locked up for the suicide attempt. I had no idea when I decided this, but I'd already chosen to not cover anything up.

"Hey, how's it going? I go by Robert." I sat down, amused by the bored-looking brunette millennial.

Instead of answering, the girl kept her eyes locked on the computer screen as if her job depended upon it. Soon, the usual questions flowed as I handed her my military ID to speed the process.

I described in embarrassing detail how I'd broken my hand, but the in-processing technician wanted nothing outside of the facts. Sticking to her script, she kept the inquiry moving along. "Are you having any thoughts of hurting yourself or someone else? Any thoughts of suicide or homicide?"

"No...well, not now," I stated playfully.

"Okay." The intake technician didn't care to ask further.

"I was an hour ago, does that count?" I made an attempt at full disclosure.

"No, you're good," she stated.

*Really? She didn't even ask whether I was suicidal or homicidal!* I actually laughed at this thought.

She looked up for the first time and almost interacted in a human manner for a brief second, before putting her mask back on. "So, just the hand?"

This was more of a statement that she wanted to be done with me than it was a question, so I gave up. "Yes, please."

Not caring, but for the reason of acceptance rather than the usual avoidance, I stood and walked to my bright red plastic chair, giggling the whole way.

Ten minutes later, John was again called to the front.

Bandaged up hours afterwards, going to my truck, I realized the trip to the hospital had been kind of fun, for some reason.

As I walked outside, I saw a huge man getting into a car two spots over from mine. Pushing 300 pounds and at least half a foot taller than me, this dude looked and dressed like the type who could've easily fit into any gang. I felt his eyes follow me as I continued to my truck, but this only amused me further.

Not long ago, mere hours in fact, I would've used this time to locate what the nearest pseudo-weapon laying around might be: a rock, a piece of metal, a bottle, anything I could use to defend myself. For some reason, though, something had changed inside me. Instead of feeling threatened, I felt the need to say hello.

*Quit living every day like you already died.* The intuitive thought was powerful, almost overwhelming. So that was what

I did. I actually walked up to the unknown man and struck up a conversation.

"Yeah, my sister's here, she got in a car accident." The stranger opened up right away.

I'd missed his name, but I didn't want to interrupt his story. I was surprised the man was so freely sharing his problems.

"I'm sorry to hear that," I empathized.

"Man, I'm not! I'm thankful, bro. That girl needs to be home with her kids, not working swing shifts! Brother, if this is going to put her where she needs to be, who cares why?"

He was kind of funny. I felt a lot, looking into his eyes. Love for family, a joy for life. Fifteen minutes later, I finally stopped asking him for more.

He then wished me well in a way that, oddly, didn't make me uncomfortable. "God bless you, bro."

I shut my door, the silence now evident to me for a different reason. It didn't feel as discomforting as usual.

*That was so strange,* I reflected, then put the manual diesel into gear with my left hand. I pulled out of the ER parking lot to the stop sign on the main road.

So much of what usually bothered me was still outside, begging for my attention, but I didn't focus on the negative, not this time. Instead, a much better understanding became the object of my attention, as I turned out onto the road and then merged onto the highway.

I hadn't eaten at all that day or the day before. In fact, I didn't remember the last time I'd eaten, but that wasn't important, either.

*He's right.* I finally knew what my top priority was, and I knew where I was headed.

Fifteen minutes later, Jacqui and my kids greeted me with relief and happiness. My wife's eyes were wondering yet kind as she somehow kept managing to put on the most beautiful smile.

*It doesn't matter why or how, just get to where you need to be...*

\* \* \*

## LAS VEGAS, NEVADA, FALL 2015

"Don't ever do that to me again, motherfucker!" Andy meant it.

Dee sat next to him, as always so thoughtful. One month after the suicide attempt, today was my first official day out of the military, so they'd flown into Vegas to surprise me. The three of us hadn't been together since Afton's funeral, almost two years before.

At the time, they were both working in a small helicopter training unit, or a unit that supported training. Whatever, it sounded awesome.

Dee usually kept an eye out for us, probably always would. When Andy's wife and her crew were killed abroad, she and other friends with influence got him reassigned from overseas directly to her back in the U.S. The stories of those two at work were beyond hilarious.

Andy sat looking straight at me for a few more seconds before he turned away and blurted out, "Fuck!"

His head twisted down and left in discomfort as he followed it up with another quiet outburst, almost as if he were sneezing in foul language. Once again, half of the people close to our table in the generic microbrew chain restaurant turned toward us.

There were no words to describe seeing my close friend like this. Afghanistan had given me PTSD, and it had given our gunner and brother Tourette's. *Maybe I should finally accept that it was that bad.*

"Fuck all of you and whatever you think," Dee asserted loudly enough for those looking to hear.

The image of a mama bear standing over her cub flashed through my mind. Actually, the vision was more like a mama bear holding a fully automatic M-4 with an underslung M-203 grenade launcher.

"I love you," I stated, using my hand to wipe my tears. "Love you both. I'm good. I promise you, I'm *not* going there again."

I was grateful to mean it, too. Dee and Andy were in town thanks to my wife. That day was my official retirement date, according to Big Blue Air Force, but I'd never bothered to arrange anything in celebration. There was no hate, no anger. I simply needed to be away from it all.

"I think about it. I think about killing myself all the time. I come home and look at my guns. I don't touch them. I just sit there and stare at them. Then I tell myself, 'Not today.'" Andy's eyes were full as he spoke his truth. "I'm not going to let my son think his dad's a fucking coward. Not today."

I knew some of this already, but not all of it. Dee sat as she listened to everything for what was clearly not the first time. It was also obviously painful for her to hear it repeated.

I'd known her since the Air Force Academy, we'd gone through flight school together. *Who could have guessed?*

We continued in silence for a while before bringing up kids, family, and, of course, Dee's husband. (If you can, picture that favorite older relative of yours. You know, the one who man-handles you too much, but you don't mind because he actually cares and always has the best stories. Yeah, her husband is that guy.)

Laughter soon took over as we picked up where we'd left off, like families do.

* * *

Andy and Dee stayed in town the one night. We wished Brack could have flown out, but I was on cloud nine seeing the two members of my crew. I loved these people more than anyone else, including most of my own family.

Seeing them also took an emotional toll that was as exhausting as a marathon. Maybe not so much seeing them, except for the sporadic crying sessions every few minutes (mostly me), but having to separate from them. Maybe it was knowing that, if there was a next time to see them, it would be a few more years, and then it would be even longer, and soon, there would be no next time.

I couldn't believe how much it still hurt to think I was no longer part of that crew.

*But he's right. We were good...* I reflected on the talks after they left.

"We were good...we were really good, you know?" Andy had stated in the backyard before we left for dinner.

This kicked off the sharing and re-telling of war stories that probably will never end.

During the early part of our deployment to Afghanistan, we'd flown with other random pilots while waiting for Dee to join us. Each temporary pilot had less of a sense of humor than the previous one.

Dee caught up to us two weeks later, but it felt like it had taken months for her to rescue us from wherever fun goes to die. Thankfully, those temp pilots left us with a lifetime of unique memories.

"Remember when Brack pulled out his knife and started to hit that pilot's helmet with it while we were flying?" Andy could barely get the words out.

All three of us called Brack our old, crusty Flight Engineer, but he was actually my age. He was just old school, growing up in Air Force Special Ops Command (AFSOC), and, like an elderly man protective of his lawn, he didn't tolerate anyone messing around with *his* aircraft.

"Holy crap, of course I do! That dude used to navigate us into a cliff wall then get pissed at me for it!" I exclaimed.

The next memory hit us at the same time. "Shit's blowing up!"

I rolled on the fake Las Vegas grass, gasping for air. I don't know if Dee snorted at this point, but I like to remember it that way. None of us were able to even sit up, we were laughing so hard at a commander who'd forgotten how to talk one day.

This officer had run up to Andy and me during one of our victory chews outside our parked bird. He must've stood there for more than a minute, his face a reddish-purple as he screamed about where everyone was.

After peeking at Andy in confusion and amusement, I spoke up for both of us. "Boss, we have no idea what you're saying..."

Our detachment commander then stopped for a few seconds, thought hard, and screamed, "Shit's blowing up!"

Instead of doing anything else, Andy and I had turned to each other and laughed our asses off just as hard the first time.

That must've finally clued him in to the correct word because he looked back up and yelled even louder over us, "*Scramble!*"

In retrospect, I guess it was only still funny to us because we weren't killed on that next mission. Our favorite aircraft, tail #204, was shot through the right engine cowling and had shrapnel throughout the rotor system. I felt a lot of pride for how I flew that day. On the other hand, I've also felt so much guilt for feeling that pride for far too long.

I wondered what it was about war. *Why do we hate it? Why do we enjoy it? Why do we hate ourselves for enjoying it?*

My crew usually didn't shoot at anyone, even when someone shot at us. I used to go through extreme fits of rage thinking about not killing that dude with the cell phone on the mountain. *Why aren't I proud, as a human being, about the times we held fire?*

We really did do everything we could for anyone who called us. And I should feel pride about helping those people. For years, I've only felt ashamed to talk about it, except for uncontrolled drunken tales and emotional outbursts.

*Why so much guilt then?* I could finally ask this question.

Days, weeks, even months after, I reflected on that visit. Dee had revealed to us that she'd gone to some voodoo witch doctor before she joined us on that deployment. Actually, I think she used the words *therapist for anxiety*, but it was the same thing to us. Being that it was her fourth trip to Afghanistan after losing so many friends, I should've paid better attention to how she'd made it through.

Andy talked about a sortie I'd tried to forget. One of the guys we pulled out of the Arghandab River Valley had died at his feet. In spite of that fact, our PJ kept up compressions and rescue breathing after calling VSA, because he wanted our other passenger, the soldier escorting our patient, to know we never gave up on his friend. How can one continue rescue breathing on a dead man?

I remembered another of our PJs collapse crying against his buddy, trying to debrief a mission in which a little girl's head had fallen apart while he was performing rescue breathing.

She'd taken metal shrapnel that had sliced her skull partly off. The skin and hair holding it together had fallen apart in his hands while he attempted to breathe life into her.

Our Pararescueman then kept breathing into this dead little Afghani girl, all while holding the pieces of her head together during the entire flight to the hospital. He did this only to make sure that her mother, sitting inches away yet isolated due to the engine noise and language barrier, would see he'd done everything he could for her daughter.

I don't know if the mother ever learned that detail or not. She might hate us regardless. What I know for sure was, that's not why our PJ was crying.

What do you call someone who does that for a stranger? A hero? Is it difficult to understand how insulting that label could be?

I still don't know how to feel about this and the many other incidents that whisper to me, inviting me back inside my memories. But I learned one powerful thing from sitting there, sharing our history with my crew.

I learned we all have horrible memories that could turn the day upside down, if allowed. But the hard ones are different for each of us, even though we were in the same events.

*Maybe this means I can learn how to see things differently, how to change my perspective?* My intuition prompted me to a new way of thinking.

Thankfully, I was able to have all of my kids in town for the Halloween weekend immediately after that visit. The noisy holiday was a welcome distraction from the emotional upheaval of the previous weeks.

By the time the weekend was over, I realized two things. First, nobody owned me anymore. Second, as a good friend later worded it, *My ladder's against the wrong wall.*

I needed to get out of Vegas. I told nobody about our move this time, and in four short weeks, Jacqui and I had the moving truck packed. I was off on a mission to find a new direction. Without acknowledging it or even making a conscious decision, for that matter, I went through a major mindset change.

I had finally decided to start living my life for my family and for me. *Now all I have to do is find that guy...*

# CHAPTER 9

# THE COURAGE TO CHANGE

**COLORADO, WINTER 2016**

N*ow what?*
So there I was, the complete opposite of fat, dumb, and happy. Instead, I found myself miserable, poor, and broken.

The most difficult part of any recovery process is most certainly *not* asking for help. Seriously, that kind of lie sets people up for failure. The most difficult part when coming to grips with mental health issues is accepting the assistance offered. Every. Painful. Moment.

One day at a time. There is no other way. That's because any good advice is only useful when applied to every situation: any behavior done out of habit, any prior judgment, any automatic reaction must be changed, one painstaking decision at a time. As a society, we crave a magic pill to solve our problems, and that is the mindset I admit to having when I went to the mental health office. Life, unfortunately, doesn't have any external solutions.

The most difficult part, for me, was also the scariest. When I finally let go of all of my excuses, every reason I had ever had to be angry, I was shocked to realize I actually couldn't stop, despite my best efforts. Becoming upset was so ingrained that it had become automatic and beyond my control. I became frightened of myself and knew just one surefire way to stop this behavior outside of death. Complete isolation.

Friends and family members became confused when I quit participating in every remaining social aspect of my life within a few months. However, the masquerade was over; I no longer had the energy to pretend things were good when they weren't. In fact, it went even deeper. I became terrified of myself.

I no longer wanted to be mad at everything and everyone, but I couldn't control my emotions. Being successful *some* of the time in social interactions was not good enough anymore. Without excuses, one single disturbing occurrence couldn't take place, let alone many of them.

This may be difficult for some to understand, but I had to re-learn a new normal for everything. The only way I'd ever been able to fit into my old life had been via focusing on impulsive behaviors and the shining moments with loved ones scattered in between that weren't tarnished by my actions.

When I began writing this book, I recognized my experiences over the previous five years had changed me in some unique ways. My entire belief structure had fallen apart, and I was still learning what that meant. For the longest time, I had difficulty doing much besides moving to the mountains of Colorado and staying indoors.

I attempted taking music classes at a nearby university but was shocked by the culture change that existed in faculty and students alike. Visions of Pink Floyd kept me amused as I put rhythm and beat to the bored glances at the clock, the heads of tired students nodding in unison, the worksheets filled out in cue to the answers given. Seemingly the only music I would find at this university was internal.

Following the third class, I stayed after to speak to my instructor. As I walked up, I watched her blow off the one other student who'd approached her. I quickly made up my mind that if the teacher was going to make herself useless, I would consider her that way too. So instead, I spoke to the kid about my original question.

In an annoyed tone, she interrupted the two of us talking about the subject matter and inquired as to whether I needed something.

Pausing, then turning, I answered her question with one of my own, "Do you know this place feels like a hospital?"

"Oh, thanks, yeah. The university just built this whole section!" The instructor lit up and wanted to go on about what was obviously important to her, aesthetics and decor.

I dismissed her values with a statement this time. "That wasn't a compliment."

I didn't care if she understood my vision of a hospital: scared, tired, silent people who did not want to be there.

*What could I learn from someone like this?* I turned my entire body again, putting myself between the other student and the teacher.

Aware I was being rude but unable to care, I spoke again to the kid on my way out the door. "Good luck with everything. I hope this is the place for you because it isn't for me."

I had no idea why, but when I got outside I felt disgusting, like I'd been walking in sewage. For some reason, the best solution I came up with was to throw my shoes away and hike four miles in the dead grass and snow to my car. All I could think was that I needed to feel something real. I don't really know why that made sense.

To top the day off, I'd gotten a parking ticket. I was parked in the farthest possible lot, yet it had also been full, so I'd parked my car on some dirt and gravel. Thankfully, the campus ticket brightened my mood, as I realized I couldn't care less and was grateful for the extra sign to take another path in life. This school wasn't for me. I crumpled up the ticket and tossed it in the trash.

As it happened, I couldn't return to college, so it was nice that I had the illusion of control for a short time. Why not? The Veteran's Administration had withheld benefits because of some obscure local university rule, and I was informed of this on the last Friday of the month (with rent due on Monday).

I'd already gone 110 days since being medically retired without any pay, disability or otherwise, because the VA was that slow. I was out of money to even buy gas. But like I said, I was grateful to be able to decide on quitting college rather than being forced to because of lack of finances.

At this point, in January of 2016, four months after being medically retired, I was also without medical benefits. I still needed more knee surgeries, but all of my referrals to orthopedic and infectious disease specialists were thrown out automatically when I transitioned out of the military. (In total, close to a dozen doctors would direct me to get further orthopedic surgery, as I was risking death or requiring amputation if I didn't have it.) I couldn't afford health insurance, and I still hadn't been in-processed into the Veterans' Administration. The clerk at the VA Clinic actually referred me to the downtown emergency room for the necessary orthopedic surgery.

*The VA hasn't in-processed me yet?* This was a troubling thought after it had been 16 months since the start of in-processing with the Medical Evaluation Board. *How much time do they need?*

The ER doctors needed me to schedule surgery with a surgeon or to come in as an emergency patient so they could perform surgery without insurance. I would need to pay a co-pay for the minimal insurance that I did have as backup, money I didn't have (because I was not being paid), and I couldn't schedule with a surgeon because the VA wasn't seeing me.

That was how I found myself at home in my own bathroom, performing my own minor knee surgery to remove infected surgical wiring that my body kept rejecting. (I must say, I did a good job, too, and had no issues for the next two months — much longer than anything prior!)

In the end, I racked up thousands of dollars in medical bills to avoid said amputation or death, all because the original surgery team had used contaminated wiring. They had implanted bacteria in the joint, which ended up taking more than 20 months to heal. I had actually tested positive for staph bacteria the week I was retired, but nobody bothered to tell me. I was finally able to see a specialist about this seven months after the test.

When I was finally in-processed by the VA, I was surprised by my new primary care physician when I asked her at the end of my appointment if she wanted to take a look at the knee. This was before the additional four surgeries I needed.

The doctor laughed as she walked out the door. "No."

I had no idea what was so funny about my question.

I had also gone into great detail discussing my suicidal history and let her know I didn't want any pills or medication. A month later, a lifetime supply of muscle relaxants, anti-anxiety pills, and painkillers arrived at my door, five prescriptions in all.

I now had the freedom to kill myself in my sleep any day of the week, for the rest of my life.

I really was let down in every single way by the Veterans Administration: financial, medical, educational, and mental health. To make matters worse, any time I requested further help, I had to prove my disability by recounting stories. Apparently benefits were only approved if I cried in front of the stranger checking off the boxes of my life.

I wanted to protest in front of the clinic, standing in my tightie-whities, holding a sign that said, *This is how you make us feel!*, but my wife refused to drive me because she didn't want me to end up in handcuffs again. (For the record, this is still an option.)

* * *

For a fairly lengthy time, I had no idea what to do or how to move forward. In other words, I found myself back at square one. No job, no possibility of ever doing the one thing I'd ever known, and no money. I searched high and low for any clues that would direct me toward a new path in life.

It was at this point that I finally surrendered to the help and guidance of others. An Air Force program reached out, bringing connections to a host of non-profits that fill in the immense VA gaps. (Please see Acknowledgements and Remarks sections for details on amazing DoD/Veteran organizations.)

I could write a separate book on the kindness of others. But to condense these experiences, I was shown that I alone could decide my future, maybe not what it would be, but how it would be. So, I decided.

I chose to quit allowing my mental health issues to control my life and learned how to ask myself the right questions. *What is the first step I can take now, no matter how small?*

I began in the only place that made sense, actively working in treatment. I took another step and began seeing two therapists. Inspired by every act of compassion shown to me, I took any step possible. I started playing music, painting, and exercising, no longer limited to when I could do something or not, but rather focused on what I could do and how to make it work.

I even tried my hand at making pottery, but to be honest, I sucked at pottery crafting. Most importantly, I learned I didn't have to enjoy all of the things I used to. There was probably a good reason why I no longer liked them, anyway.

This taught me I could challenge my previous mindsets, and I found my next question. *Why do I not like the things I used to like?*

I discovered that I had a strong desire to create for myself, instead of sitting around trying to enjoy others' work. For some reason, I also felt a calling to write, and I took it on with a passion, soon realizing how therapeutic writing could be. I even developed the beginning of several more works.

Next, I wrote song lyrics, loving that just as much, and quickly finished an album. I even began taking music classes at a college for the arts. Later, I switched to farming, quite possibly the best thing I've ever chosen to do in my life. Most of all, I learned how to keep questioning.

In the end, I needed to find one specific answer so I could accept and change my life: *Why did I put myself through so much trouble?*

In Afghanistan, I compartmentalized my experiences and emotions, just like any good pilot is supposed to do. After coming home, I suppressed everything that had been compartmentalized, consequently forcing any emotional or spiritual issue to manifest itself physically in a form of desire for alcohol, porn, sex, motorcycles — basically any adrenaline-inducing activity.

This led to further problems with impulsivity and addictions. The repetitious cycles necessitated covering up new shame and guilt, known as secondary trauma, creating a lifestyle driven by external reactions.

I further complicated my situation when I totaled an SUV with my face. A traumatic brain injury (TBI), is something I thought I was familiar with. Many of the wounded we rescued had suffered a brain injury from being blown up. In reality, I had no idea what a TBI was.

My TBI created a change in the brain that manifested symptoms similar to PTSD, and it took me much longer to figure out why I reacted so poorly to so many situations. Even when my brain finally healed, the chemical and neurological pathways had been set, so the same results kept playing out. The combination of effects from PTSD and the TBI were why I eventually pushed myself to the breaking point.

Additionally, nobody can know how different they have become following a head injury. All information is relationship-based, meaning the one way for me to know how different I had become was in relation to myself in the past. Every single undamaged, unaltered memory is all that's left of my past, and I understand all of those memories perfectly well.

Not being able to know what I no longer know (which is the same as trying to find something lost without knowing that it exists), I had no choice but to examine years of life patterns and compare them to my past to understand the true consequences of that trauma (in other words, determining how I handle similar situations then and now to determine emotional or perspective changes based upon concepts adopted post-trauma). Until doing that, I was unable to override any emotions telling me what to do (in fact, the emotional changes are so powerful that even today I struggle to go against my feelings, despite all of this knowledge and experience.)

Admitting that I am forever transformed allowed me to become functional again, giving me an understanding that the physical and emotional trauma do not have to be in control anymore. Mental health treatment can provide many different tools for recovery, but, until I was able to give input on where I wanted to go in life, treatment was just another pattern, another cycle to get stuck in.

Mental health professionals, in general, will never know the exact answers unless they've been there. This is because there is no other way to understand that the right answer varies from person to person, shaped by individual experience and perspective. Hence the need for more holistic treatment. The military doctors and counselors I went to were amazing and dedicated, but even they were limited by the unwritten rules of how much I could reveal as a pilot and what methods they could use to help me. Physiological explanations cannot do much in the moment when emotions scream otherwise. Cognitive treatment or counseling only alleviates part of the problem, leaving frustration at incomplete results in its wake.

Overall, listening to the academic-based opinions of others was never going to heal me because others had no idea what it was to have either my-specific mental disorder or brain injury. The sole way to translate theory to a new patient is through the Rosetta Stone of experience. (Once a person surrenders in full to treatment, by taking charge in some fashion, this is not necessarily true.)

You see, trauma, to a doctor, is a deeply disturbing or distressing event. Trauma, to me, means I have zero emotional memory of an event. Unfortunately, this does not translate to having no emotions when I think of the moment. Rather, the exact opposite is true. Not having an emotional memory of something means those feelings come to life in the present, not the past.

I had zero emotional memory, but internally, I was holding on to hundreds of men, women, and children who were shot, blown up, stabbed, mutilated, boiled, burned, and left fighting for life, along with many dead friends (later mostly due to suicide). And therein lies the truth.

The mind seeks to repress any trauma in order to protect itself. In combat, especially, we as humans become robotic in our behavior, sometimes unable to feel anything in the moment as a way of being able to do something in the fight to stay alive. Training and muscle memory take over while we simply act, observe, and record. Refusing to examine, question, or face the past is ultimately what results in the memories and lessons learned being hidden by the subconscious. Those lessons learned become powerful assumptions that a life is shaped around, taking the place of values, or convictions.

Jungian psychologists theorize that these experiences are what give form to our shadow, a hidden persona within the ego. More precisely, the judgments we use to develop our perception of reality, based upon concepts from the memories of those experiences, are what form the shadow.

In application, it does not matter what label is used to describe this part of a person: the shadow side, the lower self or, simply, the side that can be tempted. Generally speaking, there is a side of every person that serves no purpose but to steer them away from future trauma. This influence, similar to any bodily urge, fights harder for control in proportion to the amount of trauma suffered because of the perceived importance of personal safety. When encountering a situation similar to the trauma in any way (emotionally, physically), the mind plays out the resulting anxiety into social disasters, families in bitter dispute, and relationships torn apart.

In addition to social issues, I still struggle on many days with a lack of emotional reasoning (which, frustratingly, usually makes me feel like a toddler), but tools and tricks I've learned along the way give me a measure of peace and comfort I've not had in years. With this newfound freedom, I have been able to search for my *Why,* my reason for doing whatever I've been left alive to do.

Unfortunately, the solution for that is as unique as the circumstances it took to create my current situation. Fortunately, this question marks the exact point where life slowly grows into something better.

The beauty of free will, I've learned, is that we can choose our perspective, our reality. Before changing that, however, we must be honest with ourselves about why things are the way they are. The only way for me to do that was to face the trauma, feel the pain, and work through every single memory. And now that I have some understanding of how I got to a place of such agony, I can see things through a filter other than a fear-based lens.

So what is my perspective, my reality? For starters, I've finally accepted the fact that I'm crazy and brain damaged. I don't mope and moan a about it, though. I've accepted my own limitations, and that has given me freedom to grow beyond those limits.

Now, my life is about things I choose, no longer dictated by guilt, fear, hate, or anger. I'm able to spend time with my children, living and creating. I still don't think I will ever join a church or attend regularly. For me, organized religion, the government, and war are all too closely related. I don't see why I should ever allow another human being in an authoritative position to be involved in my spirituality.

But, in a twist, I began praying. My wife had to teach me how. Then I prayed on my own, at first in the morning and at night. When I got over how my kids acted or how anyone else judged me, I prayed at dinner. Over time, I've begun to view my every thought as a prayer. After all, whoever said that prayer officially starts with *Dear God* and ends with *Amen*?

True or not, this one idea has really opened the door for me, spiritually speaking. I still struggle with memories, and I do lose control of my emotions at times. Perhaps I always will. But I no longer hate myself for it. Now, I'm able to laugh at myself. As a result, every day has become a bit brighter. This has removed so many filters through which I used to view the world and so many false ideals I held as cornerstones of my life.

I now relate to so many people from every walk of life. Cancer survivors, ex-felons, former addicts, we really are all the same. When any of us reach an emotional or mental breaking point, we turn to our faith or our pleasure in search of whatever it is that can make us feel whole again.

The opinion of faith, as related to any other person, denomination, or religion, doesn't matter one single bit, either. The attendance sheet at wherever you publicly worship won't hold your hand through the tough times. If faith is a strong enough part of your reality, it will stand up to the storms you're called upon to weather.

If it is not, you'll continually fail and be left with nothing but blame toward everyone else until you accept responsibility for your own life and change your beliefs. These experiences will alter your behavior, your environment, your attitude, and the ideas or concepts that have caused pain and actually turn them into a source of personal strength.

My ordeals indeed became my personal strengths and led me back to my original question, *Now what?*

I realized I already had the answer when I learned the answer to my *Why*. I wish to serve others, no more, no less. Simple, right? But how could I form that into a career, or rather, a lifestyle?

Having more passion than volunteering at the local soup kitchen, I thought I'd first begin by sharing my story. It is my hope that, after reading this book, the reader may have a little more compassion for others. Perhaps a politician may begin to see decisions in a different manner, or maybe a stranger having a bad day will be granted the slightest measure of human kindness.

God willing, some of the parents and families out there who've lost loved ones to their demons may find some answers here. To that end, I extend the only wisdom I can offer to anyone who has lost another to suicide: honesty and a sincere prayer for this comparison of my experiences to be received with love.

When I pulled the trigger, my life had already made a 180-degree change from anything I'd known previously. It's there, during that change, where my story converged with that of so many other Veterans.

A lot of Veterans have problems and need help, post-combat. The unfortunate truth, however, is that many in front-line or operator positions, aircrew in my case, are not able to seek assistance. Going for mental health treatment is a huge gamble; a person's career, financial stability, medical benefits, social connections, and individual identity are immediately put on the chopping block.

As a result, many Veterans wait to seek help until after some sort of incident, legal or otherwise. For me, it was a motorcycle crash. For others, it's getting arrested, divorced, a financial disaster, or any one of myriad other things resulting from the bad judgment that follows traumatic stress.

Suppression increases the explosive possibilities, and speaking up ends personal control over the future. But for those like me, giving up control of the future is not an option. The physiological changes specifically prevent trust in others based on the perception, *I know how to stay safe, others don't.*

As soon as I made the decision to keep that control and not face the pain, I was in over my head. That's because coping strategies pop up from everywhere in the form of alcohol, drugs, sex, porn, food, gambling, and so many other things available in our society these days. Occasional, intermittent, or rotating use of these behaviors or substances will convince a person that life can be continued, so long as there is something to turn to when the desire hits. Eventually, not resorting to these vices for help demands outbursts of incontrollable anger because suppressing trauma is not a sustainable path.

Family members and friends get pushed away as quickly as they conflict with a preferred coping method, usually without knowing why. Few people in any military unit can detect what's going on with a comrade. The strange thing is, for a Veteran with an anxiety disorder, the only thing that makes sense is career and brethren.

Anytime I was in the squadron, I was the same person I'd always been to everyone there. The feeling provided almost a sense of normalcy, which aids in keeping agitation dormant, making it harder for others to recognize symptoms.

The loyalty we had to each other prevented any close friends from questioning, should they see something amiss. Having spent months or years risking our lives for each other prevented us from speaking up to the chain of command. Besides, when we all had the same look, how could any of us tell when another was locked in a downward spiral?

In the end, one glance in a friend's eyes will tell the truth: nothing is wrong with us, except that we are human. War must have this effect on people, after all, or it would never cease.

On top of everything else, many Veterans with emotional issues are embarrassed and ashamed. As an officer, a pilot, a husband, a father, a son and a friend, my behavior was unacceptable. Yet I could not stop. I became a closet addict and had no idea how, when, or why.

I played out every negative I'd ever felt toward myself, and I justified every ounce of self-hate. The misunderstood pressure from the few who cared but didn't know how to help almost always came off to me as offensive judgment.

All too often, I've heard something along the lines of, *Yeah, but...*

*Yeah, he has PTSD, but he chose to act that way...he was always kind of like that...*

Of course our loved ones are going to act in ways they have in the past, they're the exact same person! But for someone who got too drunk or did other outlandish things as a young man or woman, to restart that behavior years or decades later in adulthood, and turn an infrequent event from the hormonal young adult version of ourselves into an every-day occurrence, let me say that no, nobody with PTSD was ever like that!

*Yeah, but how much action did they really see...*

Another stigma each of us faces is nobody in this day and age could possibly live up to the hype of previous generations. I didn't scale the Eagle's Nest in 1940s Germany, nor did I single-handedly kill every bad guy while waving the American flag and saving freedom as we all know it. But, I can promise you a child doused in gasoline and lit on fire out of hatred smells just as *awful* in 2010 as it did in 1942.

In fact, every time I think or speak that word, I hear Dee's voice in my head, *Ugh, that's awful...* I don't remember how many times she said it (honestly, it might've been just the one time). But her voice is all I hear anymore in relation to that word.

At the precise moment I attempted suicide, I was convinced I was unworthy of anything and everything. I hated myself, was no stranger to death, was financially ruined, was a social outcast, and had negatively impacted every relationship within my circle of family and close friends.

To top it off, the moral injustices piled up (especially once I was introduced to the full VA experience). My classified access was pulled, my wings stripped. Overnight, I went from being over-qualified to barely employable for custodial work, land-scaping, or any other job that didn't require a dangerous tool.

No, I don't know exactly why any single person killed himself or herself. However, I'm certain I came pretty close to a generic description of many of their situations.

If you placed any Veteran in this scenario I've just detailed, station them in a random location where they have no family ties or history, and make help too costly, how could any of us expect the results to play out differently? (I believe Einstein has been credited with defining insanity as expecting different results from the same methods...yet we continue to be saddened and surprised by these specific results.)

I do know I was consumed with emotional issues no parent could eradicate, caused by perspectives no loved one could ever understand. I'm not certain when I decided suicide was the best option to solve my problems, but I became so committed to the idea that nobody could've convinced me otherwise, and there was no car fast enough to arrive in time. However, I can guarantee that, if my last thought had arrived that September day, it would've been one of regret.

* * *

I began writing this memoir with two goals in mind: improving my life and providing insight that might help heal families and relationships torn apart by lengthy wars and the countless emotional scars inflicted by them. Helping others actually seemed like the easier task at the time.

Before the suicide attempt, I'd gotten by as an impulsive prescription-addict and alcoholic. My behavior slowly woke Jacqui up to the fact that she was in the role of an unaware caregiver, and was being turned into an enabler.

Her words described our life at my lowest, "Helping Robert through this became a scavenger hunt to keep him alive."

Different obsessions had emerged as I continually searched for a lifestyle that would eliminate my anxiety. Then, I unknowingly chased my marriage in circles, as if re-building my relationship with Jacqui into something greater would undo any damage I'd caused. Multiple psychological symptoms resulted in various life patterns of spiritual bypass, addictions to projects, or emotional dependence upon others.

However, all patterns and cycles lead back to the same point in a circle. Therefore, there is no solution except to accept my changes, to externalize the negativity, to let go of that, and to break cycles through habitually *doing the opposite*, in every area of my life.

As a result, I've had to learn and practice mindfulness nearly every waking moment. It became imperative that I mentally review my emotional state and analyze every swing, on average more than once every few minutes. This can be quite maddening, but the overall results are worth it.

Despite my successes and changes, I still have dark times. The difference now is that I know how to calm myself down by getting out into nature, exercising, meditating, and praying. I was even gifted a service dog to back me up when I don't catch myself. I don't understand how a kind act such as this could've happened, but I am beyond excited to keep experiencing what my new normal feels like.

Like I mentioned, I may always struggle to handle even regular emotions, and I have no idea where I'll end up in this life. But that's not the point.

The point is, by possessing a different mindset, by choosing new perspectives, I can change anything, beginning with the patterns of my thoughts. My life is now free to improve, one step at a time. I finally understand this is what many Veterans mean by post-traumatic growth. In addition to a renewed joy for life, this growth is allowing me to shape and re-shape how I want to pursue my newfound purpose.

As for the second goal, I pray that by sharing my story, others who have lost loved ones post-combat, whether due to suicide, hospital, prison, dispute, or otherwise, may find themselves one step closer to realizing their own *Perspectives of Hope*.

Thank you for reading.

# REMARKS

**W**ould you like to know how a ground unit clears a wall for IEDs in a hurry?

The lowest-ranking grab a battering ram, like your local police might use on a front door while they are protecting and serving. Then they knock the wall over. If they don't blow up, there's no IED.

I've watched that happen over and over, in my mind. Actually, I've lived it over and over.

I don't know why, but for me, it seems the friends we almost lost stand out more than the ones we did lose. For some reason, I can make peace with the ones lost. Maybe it's because none of them will be deployed to war time and again.

Regardless of why, random triggers still take me to those *almost* times. Those times when the ground team was overwhelmed with whatever was happening, and our crew couldn't get to them fast enough.

During an earlier mission in Khandahar, our crew pushed in fast to rescue a soldier bleeding out from an IED blast. On short final of our approach, in the heart of the Black Zone, the ground commander screamed for a go-around, calling off the landing. His unit had found another IED directly under our patient. Circling once and looking for anything that resembled an alternate Landing Zone, we landed in a field to the north of the original LZ. We sat spinning on the ground, the epitome of *stuck with our pants down*, for several minutes while the PJs tried to cross a deep canal to the victim, yet were unable to.

The entire time, the ground commander kept calling us back for a casualty evacuation, so our wingman's crew landed in a field due west of the Army unit. Neither LZ was swept for IEDs, and at least one of the fields next to both had multiple mines.

This was all happening, please remember, inside an area that you did not fly over, period. In spite of this fact, we took off and orbited overhead at 100 feet, at first to provide cover. After a while, we became numb to the threat and just sat in horror as our PJs cleared the wall between them and the casualty for IEDs. I remember staring out my empty door, unable to speak because that makes a bad situation worse.

It seemed like forever that we did this, flying overhead helplessly. There was nothing to do but circle and watch to see if my friends would blow up in the field or not...along the wall or not... through the wall or not. The fear, anxiety, or whatever of where we were and the tactical stupidity of it all were so far below the fear of losing any of our team or any more of the ground unit that it wasn't a part of our decision-making process.

Those are the types of nightmares, day-mares, or memories that really hurt. Too often, I find myself looking into the past, mentally fighting to get to the fallen, staring in horror, no longer believing that prayer works.

Some readers may want more information about this mission, other missions I flew, or perhaps would've liked it if I'd included more of them. I certainly understand the passion for flying, combat, and excitement. I'd like to take this opportunity to address why I chose to write about some missions for this book and not any of the others.

The answer is simple. These missions and memories stood out the brightest in my mind before, what I thought at the time, anyway, would next be a .45 caliber bullet. The experience was not necessarily a flashback, but maybe it was. Perhaps the most accurate explanation is that my understanding of...everything... took on a different perspective from, and at, that precise moment.

To be honest, I went through many more memories, but some were unrelated and others, well, how about I say I have children and end things there? Like my death-by-vehicle attempt, it's a difficult experience to describe, and I'm left with non-descriptive bluntness as my only option to not distort my truth. Anything else added would be pure speculation.

After having much time to reflect, I suppose these memories best sum up what I had the most difficulty with. I couldn't give up the anger I had or the desire for justice. I needed revenge so I could right the wrongs I was holding onto from combat.

I've been studying a lot of spiritual writers and teachers lately. Many have referred to a timeless quote, comparing the concept of holding grudges to drinking poison and expecting your enemy to die. My struggles to find peace with these events and the memories stem from my unwillingness to accept reality. Instead, I held onto detrimental life lessons learned from those missions. My entire belief structure collapsed. I trusted nobody. I didn't care whether I lived or died.

In fact, I believed in my imminent death so much I subconsciously chose a more dangerous lifestyle at every turn of the road. Eventually that road ripped part of my face and abdomen off, while changing an unknown number of neural pathways in my brain. I now have to live with needing some kind of skill, mental tool, or outside help to overcome just about any negative emotion.

It is my hope that the reader can understand this as my greatest lesson of all. I am grateful for being this way.

I must monitor my thoughts, actions, and feelings as much as possible to avoid any episodes, fits, or as parents refer to them, temper-tantrums. For this is the best comparison of my unaware, or un-mindful self today — an emotional toddler in charge of an adult mind and body. And I am grateful for that.

I am thankful because the only cure is to always have my spirit in charge. This may sound crazy, but all it means is I must maintain my internal focus, my dedication to self and values, conditioned through mindfulness and fueled by a meditative lifestyle. I cannot dwell upon any negative emotion, ever. There isn't enough anger or negativity in the world to solve my problems. So, why bother?

For all of these reasons and more, I didn't include any of our other sorties, or flights, in this book. Nothing I did was hardcore, cool, right, or wrong. Our country chose to put the military in Afghanistan, and I chose to put myself in the military. I was in a foreign country, fighting in a war I did not, do not, and frankly, never want to understand. I did the best I could with what I had at the time.

I am proud to have been part of a crew, of a formation, that never turned around, that never said no. We repeatedly landed and/or took off under fire, sometimes having no choice but to use active minefields for LZs.

For years I've hated myself, on the deepest primal level, for any seconds I may have lost getting to the patients. Yet I always ran and flew the fastest I could to every single situation, every time. We sat and discussed tactics in our free time, figuring out how to get better as a crew. We sprinted when called, and we returned to the drawing board until we couldn't get any faster.

I am and will always be horrified by what human beings do to each other. It is just...*awful*. No, I don't have to take responsibility for one more second by holding onto my anger. Not one part of me has to ever again support a message of *taking the fight to anyone* or *getting tough!*. An outgoing commander told us to honor Wiz's death by staying, *fangs out!*. The message was clear. Badasses don't have emotional problems.

However, the things we're asked to do may lead to emotional dilemmas no matter what label our egos may desire. I consider myself ten times the person after deciding that *tough* actually means keeping a kind heart and a compassionate smile no matter the hard times.

Tough, to me, is a gunner who chose to live for the family still with him. It is a pilot who ignored every obstacle to achieve her dreams, and did everything, including asking for help, in order to still serve when those dreams became nightmares. Tough is our silent professional, a family man who was the picture of calm in every situation.

Tough, in my personal dictionary, has everything to do with how quickly we regain our human spirit and open heart after tragedy. It means maintaining love, compassion, and an awareness of our humanity in the face of pure evil. It means being able to find hope in any perspective.

Several other undertones were intentionally put into this memoir. First and foremost, I hope the lack of names in this book was apparent.

So many Afghani/Iraqi-era Veterans I speak with operated regularly on an intimate basis with smaller teams, platoons, or crews. Obviously I saw more than just my crew regularly; my undying respect, loyalty, and thanks goes out to those I was blessed to be deployed alongside. But that list, for many of us, usually stopped at around a couple dozen or so acquaintances.

As a result, anytime we had a casualty, it hit deeper than imaginable. By limiting the names in this work to my crew, my wife, and our deceased comrades, I pray my love and respect for those we lost is as transparent to readers as it is to me whenever I think of their faces.

The isolated trend of limiting who I was around continued at home, and I truly hope that pattern was also clear to the reader. From my experience getting to know other alcoholics and addicts, regardless of the individual trauma afflicting those souls, the patterns of life for a lot of them become similar.

I say, *regardless of trauma*, because at some point, the problems we face are all of similar origin. Whether suppressing traumatic experiences from war, poverty, drugs, abuse, neglect or simply being taught to deny emotions, the results are the same. By repressing feelings of hurt and pain, we become closer to our faith or closer to our addictions.

Whatever *It* is to each of us, that is what we will be drawn to. We only have to look within to find that the real answer to what *It* is, is the same as the question *Why*.

In our society, many people bounce from one minor addiction to another so frequently, with *just enough* time for moderation in between, that they never introspectively search for that answer. The result is many of us can live long lives without ever realizing how close to addictions we may come, at least during one point or another in life.

This might not be as apparent a theme, but I truly wish to encourage others who are having problems just trying to stay afloat. It is possible to jump off the impulse rollercoaster any time we choose. The uncertainty of what lies next may appear terrifying at first. But in another perspective, that discomfort of the vast unknown is what endless possibility feels like. That is true freedom.

Otherwise, the need for those other things distorts any awareness of the actual need for growth on a spiritual level. Those urges to let loose or unwind, as they may typically be masked, will find a way to influence every choice we make in life. By spiritual level I am not referring to religion, but rather faith in something greater that ultimately results in faith in one's self.

Faith in one's self ultimately taught my final Afghani lesson: There is only one message worth remembering, one lesson worth learning, one way of living after war, trauma, or loss: Love. Seeing the love in any experience or situation is all that matters.

Sometimes we must fight; sometimes we must defend ourselves. That is a fact of life. Bad things can happen to good people. But we cannot remain fixated upon these things.

Somehow, even war has become a constant in our society. At the time this book was written, war has become background noise, an assumptive necessity. In far too many ways, warfare has become an industry. After all, there has never been any true finish line. Controlling "Hearts and Minds", in actuality, is one step shy of fighting imagination.

I am not anti-war, nor am I pro-war. I am pro-Veteran. I only wish to share my opinion that the returns have not been matching our investments. In too many areas I witnessed, we were solving problems created mostly by our presence.

Every service member is a volunteer. He or she will go any-where, at any time, in whatever condition, for as long as neces-sary. And they'll go back, too. I trust that everything happens for a reason, so no, I don't think that a single effort or sacrifice has been in vain. But I do hold the belief that, for the dedication of these Veterans, any time we send our service members any-where, it better be absolutely necessary.

Actions from handfuls of non-state actors have resulted in massive, seemingly endless, worldwide deployments. The only visible overall objective is an insubstantial desire to reset vari-ous cultural dispositions toward western society in general. In this floating, emotionally-relative timeline, have we lost our own perspective on reality?

We set the boundaries, the conditions, the combatants, and the finish line (or lack thereof). Right or wrong, our way of war, to include conducting it or not, is clearly our choice.

After so many years, now decades, why aren't we capable of choosing better? Is it because we keep war to such small scales that not enough understand the true effects? Do any of us actu-ally want to leave our kids a future including this never-ending warfare, as kind of a twisted inheritance?

War, hate, fighting, or addictions can never become a way of life, or even a consistent part; they will only destroy. Anything in between these things and a life dedicated to love will lead to fruitless, never-ending searching, no matter how sweet the sugar may seem in the moment.

An old French expression teaches, *Tout comprendre c'est tout pardonner*. To understand all is to forgive all.

Maybe this is why love is so powerful. Every emotion, event, or sensation has a polar equal: For every Good, there's a Bad, for every Happy, a Sad. Fun vs. Boring, Soft or Abrasive, every Party eventually turns into a Hangover. They each have another side to their magnetic selves. To be drawn towards one end of a spectrum implies an eventual return to center, a suggested, to-be-experienced reverse of what lifts us up. But love is different. Because of the very nature of love, that undefinable human quality, it encompasses understanding and forgiveness of all. Love truly is the sole lesson worth living.

After all, Love has no opposite.

*Our crew, Andy, Dee, Brack, and myself. Camp Bastion. Fall, 2010.*

*Me hanging out with maintenance right before crew swap. Camp Bastion. Fall, 2010.*

*Dee landing into a Helmand brownout. Fall, 2010.*

*Me (not flying) over Helmand. Fall, 2010.*

*Brack Flying over Khandahar. Summer, 2010*

*Andy loading ammo cans in Helmand. Fall, 2010.*

*PJs view. Khandahar. Summer, 2010.*

*With so many patients to pickup after a dust storm, we found our-*
*selves having to wait as #3 for landing at the hospital pad. Each*
*aircraft was carrying Cat Alphas from the Arghandab River Valley.*
*Khandahar. July, 2010.*

*On a few flights, we were able to get high enough to take photos.*
*Arghandab River Valley. Summer, 2010.*

*The Arghandab River Valley. Summer, 2010.*

*FE calling an approach. Khandahar. Summer, 2010.*

*PEDRO Maintenance work the night on Tail #204 following .762 caliber damage over Arghandab. Our maintainers were so good at keeping these things going that they were able to combine regular phased inspections/repairs with the ground fire down-time and get it back to us the next morning. Khandahar. July, 2010.*

*Memorial in the Maintenance Hangar for PEDRO 66. Our sister ship went down over the town of Sangin, Helmand Province. Camp Bastion, Summer, 2010.*

*PEDRO Patch. A Vietnam-Legacy Rescue Callsign, this was worn almost as a badge of honor.*

# ქართული 32-ე საშშვიდობო ბატალიონი
## 32nd GEORGIAN ARMY BATTALION

## CERTIFICATE OF APPRECIATION
### მადლობის სერთიფიკატი

**WORKHORSE**

TO PEDRO

მოცს 32-ე ბატალიონის სახელით
ვადგაც-იბაცდით ელრძესი მადლიობა
ვაძოინწყელი სამსახურის და
მზარდაჭენრისათვის. თქვენ დადიაუდედელი
სამსახური გასწიეთ, რათა 32-ე ქართულ
ბატალიონს ჰებქჭერად შეესრულებდას
დაკისრებული მისია. თქვენ იყავით ჩვენი
ბატალიონის ორგანული წევრი ჩვენ
ვადიებდთ თქვენს დავწლს და
ბატალიონის სახელით ვისურვები
ბედნიერებას ჯარდ ცხოვრებაში და
წარმატებას კარიერაში.

ყ... ლობაც
32-ე ბატალიონას მეთაური
    პ. ტერელაძე
უფრ. სერჟანტი   მ. ნიკოლაძე
32-ე ბატალიონის სერჟანტი

TO PEDRO

On behalf of the 32nd Georgian Battalion
assigned to Regimental Combat Team 8 would
like to thank you for your outstanding
dedication, service and support. You have truly
made a positive impact on the battalion mission
accomplishment successfully. You were our
battalion organic member during our deployment
and we highly estimate your merit. On behalf of
the Georgian battalion I wish you success in
your future service.

LTcolonel     P. TERELADZE
Commanding 32nd Georgian battalion
First Sergeant    M. NIKOLADZE
Battalion Sgt of The 32nd Georgian battalion

დელერამში, ავღანეთი
DELARAM, AFGHANISTAN
2011

*Two of the thank you letters from allied units our crews and teams helped (the second, on pages 226-227, was reconstructed due to poor picture quality). Helmand. Summer, 2010.*

B-COY
ISAF 9
DABG

Date

10 august 2010

To all PEDRO operators

On behalf of all soldiers in the 3rd armoured infantry platoon, BRAVO company, The Royal Guard Regiment, The Royal Danish Army

We would like to extend our deepest and most heartfelt thanks to all the people involved with the PEDRO callsigns.

On numerous occasions have we had the privilege of your help, and Saturday August 7th will forever be one we will remember with sadness, but also memories of appreciation and awe towards the help you provided us with.

At approximately 11.00 am on this Saturday, a huge IED blew platoonleader 1st Lieutenant ██████████'s infantry fighting vehicle upside down, on the road that connects the patrol bases on the PB Line. Of all 7 soldiers on board, one soldier was instantly killed while all others but one, suffered severe injuries. While others refused, PEDRO landed close to the wreck, and aided us in caring for our comrades, and taking them to the fieldhospital in Camp Bastion. The gunner was trapped in the turret for hours, and we lost hope of him surviving for every minute that passed. PEDRO operators with special cutting equipment landed and offered their assistance, never leaving the area, and never letting us know that they would leave us or our comrade. Eventually, a recovery vehicle made it possible for us to reach our mortally wounded gunner; but by then it was clear that he had passed. The PEDRO operators, in the most respectful and caring manner, offered to remove the body of our hero, so that we would remember him as he was alive. These were the words used by the operator. Knowing what morale means to fellow soldiers, this deed is forever remembered by all of us. Putting his body in a bodybag, you asked for our nations flag to wrap around him, honouring him, and honouring all of us. You then offered our soldiers to take our friend to your helicopter.

We will certainly miss our two lost brothers, but the rest will survive, which is the result of the work done by both our soldiers, but also very much by the pilots, medics, operators and soldiers of the PEDRO callsigns.

You are an inspiration to us, and your professionalism knows no limits. Thank you so very much, we are privileged to have such allies.

Sincerely yours

SFC Christian Bøgekjær
Platoonsergeant
3rd armoured PLT

All 3rd PLT soldiers

*For many of us, these thank you's will forever outweigh any other military award, medal, or recognition. Helmand. Summer, 2010.*

## AIR FORCE WOUNDED WARRIOR PROGRAM

The Air Force Wounded Warrior Program is a Congressionally-mandated, federally-funded program that provides personalized care, services and advocacy to seriously wounded, ill or injured Total Force recovering service members and their Caregivers and families. AFW2 focuses on specific personal and family needs and includes programs that cover a gamut of situations throughout the recovery process and beyond.

This is a legal way of saying that AFW2 stuck with my family through it all. Adaptive sports, art therapy, music therapy, nutrition classes, financial management, job fairs, VA assistance, connections within my local veteran community, training/connections with fellow Veteran mentors, an Ambassador speaking group, and a new kitchen sink (just kidding) are some of the ways they help Veterans. In addition, AFW2 and their DoD Service counterparts annually organize The Wounded Warrior Games, formal training, and representation at The Invictus Games.

"Generational Impact" truly describes what the beautiful people associated with this program do for a living.

To find out more or to help, please visit:

**www.woundedwarrior.af.mil**

*Jacqui and I in a Rock to Recovery performance. Music therapy during AFWW Events is an uplifting, energetic experience run by Rock to Recovery and their rad group of musicians.*

## ROCK TO RECOVERY

Rock to Recovery's mission is to transform lives via the powerful, healing, consoling experience of music. Through our musical programs, Rock to Recovery gives people hope where there may be hopelessness and shows people light where there is darkness.

Former (hed) P.E. and Korn guitarist Wes Geer founded Rock to Recovery in 2012 in an effort to bring a new and unique type of music expression group into treatment -by forming a band! Together with Rock to Recovery's staff of professional musicians, the band writes and performs a song, finally recording it at the end of each session.

They bring fun into treatment and recovery by offering a natural escape from the fear-based mind. This helps people grow a sense of belonging and self esteem. They help to vent emotions by writing lyrics and singing together for release, in real-time. A positive theme of hope in recovery is tied in throughout the whole process. When the session is done, "band" members feel a new energy all throughout their minds and spirits.

Music is a powerful tool, proven to help soothe the soul. For someone in recovery, learning to have clean and sober fun, feeling a part of, connecting to a group, and quieting the mind are keys to a successful new life. It's time to feel good in all that we do.

To find out more or to help, please visit:

**rocktorecovery.org/donate/**

*Wesley Geer of Rock to Recovery and formerly of Korn each week interviews rad musicians, rockstars, celebs, people, that have overcome their demons. Wes recently invited me to join this special group of volunteers speaking on behalf of helping others through personal testimonies.*

*Please check out the podcasts at:*

**rocktorecovery.libsyn.com**

*Rock to Recovery Radio interview. Laguna Beach, CA. Spring, 2018.*

*Jacqui, me, and Wes.*

## WOUNDED WARRIOR PROJECT

The mission of the Wounded Warrior Project® (WWP) is to honor and empower Wounded Warriors. Our vision is to foster the most successful, well-adjusted generation of wounded service members in our nation's history.

"In less than a year of being out of service, I had transferred nearly every personal mental health recovery or treatment of mine into a program run, financed by, or referred through your outstanding non-profit. Personal therapy, individual Veteran trips, marriage retreats, family events, and an intensive outpatient PTSD/TBI program have helped transform my 'Why' into 'How.'"

To find out more or to help, please visit:

**www.woundedwarriorproject.org**

## OPERATION MEND

The mission of Operation Mend is to partner with the United States Military to jointly heal the wounds of war by delivering leading-edge patient care, research, and education and using the best medicine and technology available. The vision is to heal humankind, one patient at a time, by improving health, alleviating suffering and delivering acts of kindness. It is an honor and a privilege to serve members of the United States Military and their families. Our values ensure integrity, compassion, respect, teamwork, excellence, and discovery while recognizing that every patient and family is unique.

All funding for the care of our wounded warriors and their families comes from the support of grateful Americans.

For my wife and I, WWP were those Americans—Operation Mend is just one of many mental health treatment programs that WWP funds for post-9/11 Veterans.

To find out more or to help, please visit:
**www.uclahealth.org/operationmend/**

## VETERANS' TO FARMERS

The mission of Veterans to Farmers is to train veterans in agricultural systems, technologies, and business operations for a fulfilling and sustainable lifestyle.

Veterans to Farmers offers an opportunity for our men and women who have sacrificed so much to be our protectors. We offer a way to recover, to learn, and to move forward by becoming our providers, contributing to the solution of our food insecure nation.

To find out more or to help, please visit:

**www.veteranstofarmers.co**

## ELIZABETH DOLE FOUNDATION

*Jacqui with Senator Elizabeth Dole at the Dole's private residence. Washington D.C. Fall, 2018.*

The Elizabeth Dole Foundation's mission is to strengthen and empower America's military caregivers and their families by raising public awareness, driving research, championing policy, and leading collaborations that make a significant impact on their lives.

Senator Dole's Foundation gives military and veteran caregivers a voice, an option to do the right thing by helping provide input to make changes. But even more importantly, they gave Jacqui a community, fun, and friendship. She was valued, respected, and allowed to help others in a way that is simply unmatched, worldwide.

To find out more or to help, please visit:

**www.elizabethdolefoundation.org/**

## ROSALYN CARTER INSTITUTE FOR CAREGIVING

Rosalyn Carter Institute for Caregiving establishes local, state, national, and international partnerships committed to building quality, long-term, home and community-based services. We believe this begins with providing caregivers with effective supports to promote caregiver health, skills and resilience. We also believe strongly in the need to provide greater recognition for professional and family caregivers. We focus on helping caregivers coping with chronic illness and disability across the lifespan.

To find out more or to help, please visit:

**www.rosalynncarter.org**

## HELPFUL ORGANIZATIONS

**Semper Fi Fund/America's Fund** is dedicated to providing immediate financial assistance and lifetime support to post-9/11 combat wounded, critically ill and catastrophically injured members of all branches of the U.S. Armed Services and their families. We deliver the resources they need during recovery and transition back to their communities, working to ensure no one is left behind.

To find out more or to help, please visit:
**semperfifund.org**

**Wounded Warrior Family Support's** mission is to provide support to the families of those who have been wounded, injured or killed during combat operations. The families of our casualties suffer in many ways: some financially, some psychologically.

To find out more or to help, please visit:
**www.wwfs.org**

**Our Military Kids, Inc.** is a 501(c)(3) nonprofit organization that supports children (ages 5–12th grade) of deployed National Guard and Reserve service members, as well as those of wounded veterans from all service branches, with grants that cover up to six months of a chosen activity. Participation in these extracurricular activities has proven to help military children cope with stress and anxiety, as well as foster a sense of self-confidence and positivity, while their parents are recovering or serving overseas.

To find out more or to help, please visit:
**ourmilitarykids.org**

**Operation Homefront** is a national 501(c)(3) nonprofit whose mission is to build strong, stable, and secure military families so they can thrive — not simply struggle to get by — in the communities they have worked so hard to protect. For over fifteen years, we have provided programs that offer: RELIEF (through Critical Financial Assistance and transitional housing programs), RESILIENCY (through permanent housing and caregiver support services) and RECURRING FAMILY SUPPORT programs and services throughout the year that help military families overcome the short-term bumps in the road so they don't become long-term chronic problems.

To find out more or to help, please visit:
**www.operationhomefront.org**

**Hearts of Valor**™ seeks to honor the service and sacrifice of the people who care for our nation's wounded, ill or injured warriors by providing a community of support based on a foundation of empathy and mutual understanding.

To find out more or to help, please visit:
**www.heartsofvalor.org/**

**Quality of Life Foundation** strives to make positive differences in peoples' lives today that will continue far into the future. By focusing on initiatives that improve the quality of life of those who have been struck by misfortune, and teaching them skills for rebuilding in spite of those life struggles, the Foundation will have indeed provided a life-long benefit to those they serve.

In March 2010, the Quality of Life Foundation launched the Wounded Veteran Family Care Program to support families who provide a substantial amount of care giving to a wounded, injured or ill veteran. Our client families include veterans with combat and non-combat-related traumatic brain injuries; PTSD, stroke; spinal cord injuries; multiple amputations; and other poly-trauma injuries. The Quality of Life Foundation focuses on the whole family because often times, care giving responsibilities, coupled with financial strain, result in family members forgoing their own quality of life needs. Things like recreation, respite, home modifications, house and lawn care, and personal care (haircuts, medical and dental appointments, etc) take a low priority due to income and time constraints. We address quality of life needs through local and national resources, or through the outright purchase of goods/services.

To find out more or to help, please visit:
**woundedveteranfamilycare.org**

**Center for American Military Music Opportunity (CAMMO)** has a mission to create music-based therapeutic programming and outlets for service members, veterans and family members; To train and educate service members, veterans, and their families in music career opportunities including artist development.

This organization believes in the power of music to restore, inspire, and open doors to our veterans and service members. With that said, the financial contributions of our donors have been a tremendous help and we ask for your continued support as the services rendered by CAMMO expand. If you've never given, we ask that you consider the life-changing effects your gift will have on a U.S. veteran or service member suffering from PTSD or TBI. Every dollar counts!

To find out more or to help, please visit:
**www.cammomusic.org**

**Team R4V's** mission is to support the rehabilitation of and provide opportunities for veterans in the United States through their involvement in athletics, races and adaptive sports.

Team Racing for Veterans (Team R4V) is on a journey of giving back to America's heroes. Specifically, Team R4V fosters a commitment to veterans by promoting awareness, supporting rehabilitation, and empowering individuals to follow through on a path of healing with a sense of pride and accomplishment. Through the unique power of athletics, we aim to help disabled veterans not just get well, but get better- achieving more than they ever thought possible.

To find out more or to help, please visit:
**www.teamr4v.org**

**The Cohen Veterans Network** seeks to improve the quality of life for veterans, including those from the National Guard and Reserves, and their families. CVN works to strengthen mental health outcomes and complement existing support, with a particular focus on post-traumatic stress. Our vision is to ensure that every veteran and family member is able to obtain access to high-quality, effective care that enables them to lead fulfilling and productive lives. CVN is a registered 501c3 Private Foundation.

To find out more or to help, please visit:
**www.cohenveteransnetwork.org**

# ABOUT THE AUTHOR

Robert grew up in small town Georgia, admittedly more interested in sports and the outdoors than academics. He graduated high school in 1998, attended Marion Military Institute from 1999-2000 and earned a Bachelor of Science from the United States Air Force Academy in 2003.

Earning the rank of 2nd Lieutenant at graduation, Robert went on to flight training, first at Vance AFB, then being awarded his pilot wings at Ft Rucker, AL, in 2005. Throughout his career, he flew over 1500 flight hours as a UH-1N Instructor Pilot and a HH-60G Pilot. Diagnosed with Post Traumatic Stress Disorder and a Traumatic Brain Injury, he was medically retired at the rank of Major in 2015, after 12-1/2 years of service.

Major Scoggins is a combat Veteran of Balad AB Iraq; Khandahar Airfield and Camp Bastion, Afghanistan; and Camp Lemmonier, Djibouti, Horn of Africa.

As a HH-60G Combat Rescue Pilot, he conducted 252 Combat Missions, totaled 291 Rescued/Recovered, and 151 Lives Saved. Over 200 of those missions and almost all of the 291 Americans, allies, and civilians were in Afghanistan, 2010.

Robert is married to Jacqueline Scoggins and is the proud father to four uniquely creative and beautiful children. He lives with his family in Colorado where he gets by as a full-time dad, and a part-time writer, speaker, painter, farmer, and entrepreneur.

*Perspectives of Hope* is the first work by Major Robert Scoggins, USAF, ret.

Robert can be reached for public events and speaking engagements at PerspectivesOfHope.com